Norwich Lives:
selected graves from Earlham Cemetery

Françoise Donovan

Norwich Lives: selected graves from Earlham Cemetery

First published 2013
by Elysé Publications.
granouche40@gmail.com

Copyright © 2013 Françoise Donovan.
All rights reserved. No part of this publication may be copied, reproduced, stored in a retrieval system, or transmitted, in any form or by any means, electronic, mechanical, photographic, recording or otherwise, without the prior written permission of the publisher.

Publication design by John King.
Printed by Page Bros., Norwich.

ISBN: 978-0-9926773-0-5

Acknowledgements and thanks

Many friends have contributed thoughts and advice to this book.
I want to thank them all for stepping in, often at short notice, at various stages of the redaction or in the field.

I also want to thank John Donovan for his interest and constructive criticism and my daughter, Mahalia Millett for her encouragement.
Special thanks go to my son, Joël Donovan, for his constant support and thoughtful contributions and to my friend, Rosemary Le Fevre, for her indefatigable help on all fronts.

Jeremy Bartlett; Jackie Brown; Alan Churchyard for Rosetta Soman; Maureen and David Cubbitt for Douro Potter; Clare Everett; Alison Gibson for Joshua Pearce; Judith Havens for the extra information about John Abel; Stu Haats; Laurence Heyworth; Simon Jackson; John King; Judith Walzer Leavitt; Lisa Little; Jan Melichar; Daisy Njoku; Annie Ogden; John Renton; Mark Rudd of Norwich City Hall for the map and location of various graves; Valerie Simms; Caroline Smith; William Swainger; Christine Wilson and Diane Wilson. Staff from various libraries and museums.

Thanks also to all those I have met in the course of writing this book who have generously offered the information they had.

Cover picture: Frances and John Abel memorial. (Photo by Bill Smith)

Contents

Acknowledgements 2
Preface 5
In the beginning 7
A pain so deep 9
A woman's place in life and death 12
Douro Potter 16
The Caleys 18
Daniel Sayer 22
Buried above their station? 27
Ann Mussett 31
Amenaide Vulliamy 35
The Greens and the Markwells 38
George Skipper 41
Rosetta Soman 43
Sarah Rice 46
Kiyoshi Hata 49
Casualties of war 51
Henry Firth 55
Joshua Pearce 58
Man proposes, God disposes –
   Eliza Stevenson, Mary Ann Taylor,
   Albert Forster, Wladzilaw Slizewski,
   Eugenia Zagajewska, Isengelo Masudi et al ... 62
Let their loved ones speak 71
Conclusion 85
Notes 86
Bibliography 87
Picture credits 88
Location map 90

*To my grandchildren Esmée and Adam
who have yet to comprehend mortality.*

Preface

The graves in this book form an eclectic selection – some chosen for the beauty of their headstones, some for the interest of their inscriptions, others for the significance of their occupants.

In my frequent visits to the cemetery, I noticed at times an attractive design or a touching epitaph; at others a strange name or an intriguing set of dates. The more I got to know the grave itself, the more I wanted to know about its occupant.

As Pozzo says in Beckett's *Waiting for Godot*: *"They* [our mothers] *give birth astride a grave, the light gleams an instant, then it's night once more"*.

As well as being constantly reminded of the ephemeral nature of the human passage on earth, I became aware of the fragility of the monuments that we erect to those taken from us. I could see that many graves and inscriptions were disappearing fast and I felt compelled to extend their life somehow; often very little is left of the original inscription, or the decoration, although the headstone is still standing. Sometimes the whole grave has fallen to pieces. This is my very modest attempt to preserve on paper some of those monuments which time and tide must eventually erase.

This little deer is all that is left of a now anonymous grave.

This ethereal Christ will soon be totally invisible.

These portraits on the partly collapsed grave of an Italian couple are now lying on the ground, at the mercy of lawnmowers and other hazards.

I apologise for any errors occasioned by my need to use a degree of intuition and imagination to interpret the evidence available, which is often circumstantial, about these long-deceased people.

In the beginning

Publicly-funded cemeteries were an innovation of the 19th century. Most of them were built in the 1850s and 1860s, to comply with successive government burial acts. These were passed because a link had been established between overflowing city churchyards and epidemics, especially cholera (there was a cholera epidemic in 1848-9 which affected Norwich). The Norwich (Earlham) cemetery, set in 34 acres of land, was designed by Edward E Benest, the City Surveyor, to cater for all faiths, with some consecrated sections for Church of England burials and unconsecrated ones for non-conformists.

There is a separate chapel and burial ground for Jews. There is also a large section for Catholics and a growing one for Muslims as well as two military cemeteries. Part of the grounds were designed in the more informal style of the so-called 'garden cemeteries' with winding pathways. But most of it is of the grid type which was favoured by the doyen of cemetery designers, John Claudius Loudon (1783-1843) because it is more economical, with a better use of space. The result is a pleasant mix of graves and trees, in keeping with Loudon's recommendations: he saw them as *'instructive, educational and soothing places'.*

James Baldry, aged 32, was injured while erecting scaffolding during the construction of the chapel and he died on 20th December 1855. He had the sad privilege of being buried before the cemetery was officially opened on 1st March 1856.

In the first ten months of its opening 745 burials took place but only four of the mourning families could afford a headstone. Burials themselves cost five shillings for a first class and two shillings for a fourth class burial, when the weekly wage of an agricultural labourer was about nine shillings. These prices did not include the erection of a stone or the purchase of a plot. The

19th and early 20th century graves and memorials which are still visible are the more affluent tip of a huge iceberg of invisible residents made up of those who couldn't afford a stone or even a paid burial.

Two superintendents looked after the cemetery. One was for the established Church, living in North Lodge; the other was for non-conformists living in South Lodge, both rent-free. They also assisted in the digging of graves and were paid £1 per week plus two shillings per grave. *James Self*, superintendent for 27 years, is buried near North Lodge where he lived.

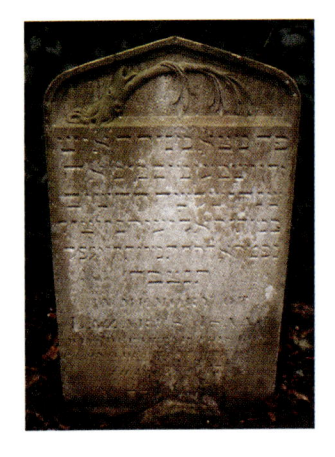

One of the first occupants of the cemetery, who died on 22nd June 1857, is also the one reaching back furthest in time: *Lazarus Isaac* died aged 100 and is buried in the Jewish cemetery. He was born in 1757, about a hundred years after the Jews re-established themselves in England, encouraged by Oliver Cromwell. There is evidence of Jews in Norwich in the late 18th century, working as apothecaries, upholsterers and silversmiths, but they amounted to only about 20 families. One Levy Isaac, a silversmith, is described in 1780 as 'long resident in this city'. He could well be Lazarus's father.

In 1893 the Eastern Daily Press reported that 'peaceful occupant' number 57,759 had just been buried. That number was equivalent to more than half the inhabitants of Norwich at the time. Today the number of 'peaceful occupants' is in the hundreds of thousands and the shortage of burial space is acute; although increasing use of cremation can partly alleviate the problem, it cannot solve it. A section of the cemetery, including the crematorium and adjacent memorial garden, was sold in 1998 and is now run by Dignity plc. (Note 1)

A pain so deep it will never heal . . .

Anyone looking at inscriptions on gravestones will be struck by the repeated occurrence of spouses following each other to their graves.

It is well-known that when one of an old couple dies, the other tends not survive very long. The most extreme example in Earlham Cemetery is that of *William* and *Susan Youngs*. William died first, aged 79, on 28th February 1892. Susan survived him by only a few hours. There is no record of them having been involved in an accident. *Charles Thurston* died in May 1969 aged 72; *Lilian*, his wife died in October 1969 aged 71. In a cemetery you soon realise that this tendency seems to be the case for couples of all ages, not just the aged ones.

In recent years, various studies have revealed the existence of 'heart-broken syndrome'. A major one undertaken by Harvard University researchers in 1993 and lasting nine years concluded that *"grieving spouses have higher long term risk of dying from strokes and heart attacks"'* . (Note 2). It seems, in other words, that in line with popular belief, you can die of a broken heart.

There has been no such systematic research on the incidence of other illnesses like cancer or multiple sclerosis in the recently bereaved. However, bereavement counsellors are aware that many people suffering from a significant loss develop physical diseases resulting in premature deaths – even though those deaths may not appear directly related to grief. As anyone who has been bereaved knows, the overwhelming pain of loss seems at times to exceed the ability of the body to cope with it. As Shakespeare put it, *"The grief that does not speak knits up the o'er wrought heart and bids it break"*. (Note 3)

Of the many graves in the cemetery falling under this rubric, these are a few of the most striking examples:

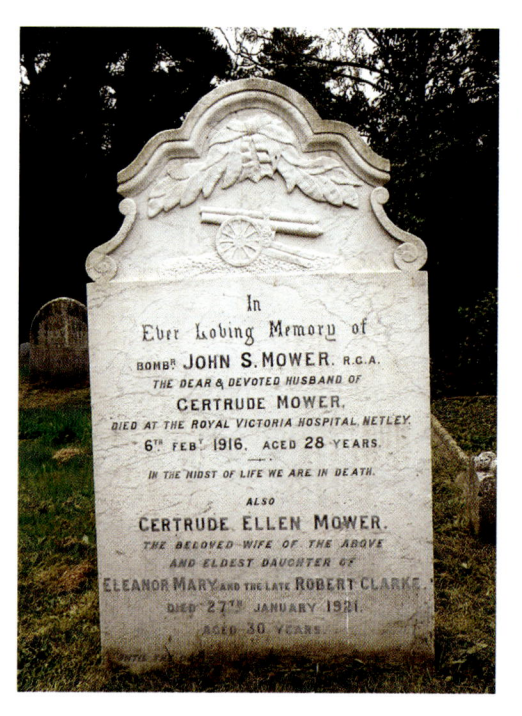

John Mower, a Bombardier injured in the First World War. He died at Netley Military Hospital, aged 28, soon after his arrival there, in 1916. His wife *Gertrude* followed him five years later aged only 30.

Albert Smith was killed by enemy action on 29th April 1942; his wife *Kathleen* died suddenly in 1945.

It is not just spouses, but mothers and fathers:

Ann Burcham died in October 1859, aged 19. Her brother *George* died in December 1861 aged 16. Their mother *Ann* died in April 1863 aged 53.

Frederick Jarrett died aged 23 in July 1917. His father died five years later aged 58. Frederick was his only son.

Many babies and small children did not long survive their mothers' deaths:

Edith Humphrey died in childbirth at 25 on 28th September 1901; her daughter *Eva*, died in March 1902 aged 5 months.

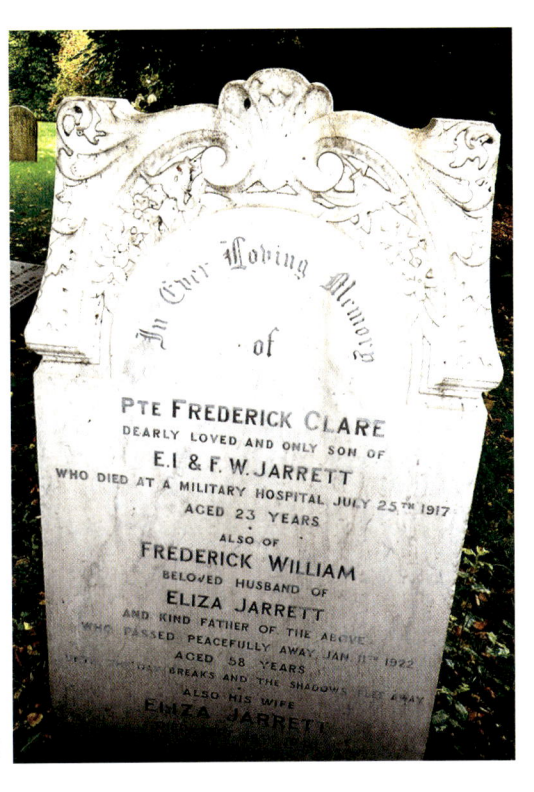

Alice Rogers died on 13th December 1881 aged 24; her son *Robert* a month and a half later aged 15 weeks.

Christine Sexton, who died in 1904, speaks for all dying mothers in this heart-rending epitaph:

*Farewell dear husband,
my life is past
you loved me faithful till the last
grieve not for me,
not sorrow make
but love our child for my sake.*

A woman's place in life and death

In some ways the world of the deceased reflects the world of the living that they used to inhabit. The memorial stones of women buried in the 19th or early 20th century speak eloquently of how they fared in male-dominated society.

The law, institutions, families and individuals all treated women as second-class citizens and inferior beings. The Matrimonial Causes Act of 1857 gave men the right to divorce adulterous wives, but a husband's infidelity was to be endured. In any case, after a divorce children were the father's property and he could (and often did) stop the mother from seeing them.

And yet, on the whole, middle-class women had to marry, whether they wanted to or not, for economic reasons. If they didn't they would be a burden, first on their parents and then on their brothers, because there was no suitable work for them except as governesses or teachers, both unglamorous and badly remunerated occupations. Even midwifery was barred to women by the male medical establishment from 1840 onwards (see page 46).

So the only acceptable career choice was marriage, upon which all a wife's power, property and indeed legal identity went to her husband to deal with as he saw fit, until the law was eventually changed in 1882 with the Married Women's Property Act. A remarkable illustration of the extreme consequences of the pre-1882 law is the case of *Jane Burrell*, a minor, who during the Christmas school holidays left Norwich for Fakenham and was kidnapped by her two uncles, brothers *Frederick* and *Henry Burrell*. The next day, 20th January 1863, Frederick, having taken Jane to Woolwich, married her, unbeknown to her mother and Jane's guardian. The motive? Jane had suddenly become heir to real estates in Norfolk on the death of her grandfather, Daniel Burrell. The uncles were tried and convicted for having *"fraudulently allured, taken and detained"* her. Unabashed, they appealed and the Court of Appeal *'with very great regret'* quashed the conviction. (Note 4)

Women were largely powerless to change their status as they didn't have the right to vote until 1928.

On a typical Victorian gravestone a woman's first name is given followed by 'wife of', or 'wife of the late', or in the early and mid-19th century 'relict of', then the full name of the husband, perhaps with an indication of where he came from and his position. Her maiden name is not given. The word 'relict' is shocking to modern sensibilities. From the Latin relinquere, to leave behind, it describes a widow as someone left, left behind, perhaps even left over, which brings to mind the Hindu custom of Sati – where the 'left-over' widows were burnt alive on the funeral pyre.

These are two examples from the mid-Victorian period and early twentieth century:

Anne, relict of the *Rev Thomas Talbot*, late rector of Tivetshall, in this county †1868.

Edith Bessie Jane, wife of *A.R. Anderson CBE* and daughter of *Charles Tuck* J.P. of Blofield †1928.

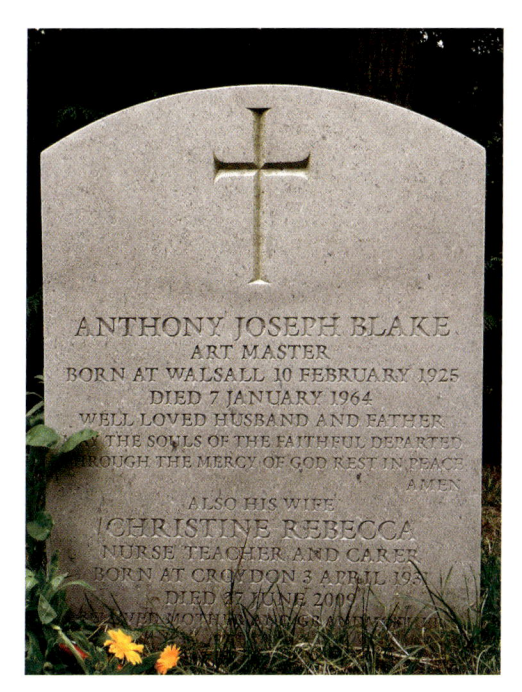

In contrast, two inscriptions from the late 20th century show that grave inscriptions now tend to reflect women's achievements in their own right:

Anthony Joseph Blake, Art Master, born at Walsall, †1964. Also his wife Christina Rebecca, nurse, teacher and carer, born at Croydon †2009.

*Mary Eileen Chambers nee Walker †2006. A devoted wife to Bob and dedicated mother to her children.
A woman of great strength, endurance and commitment.
Who held all her children dear to her heart.*

The reflected status awarded to deceased women through association is also a feature of the inscription on the grave of a manservant William Ashmore:

> *For many years the
> Faithful servant of the Revd
> Sir Edward Pepps Jodrell
> Baronet of Salle Park
> in this county
> † 1871 (52 yrs old)*

We are told more about his master than about him.

Douro Potter
†1925

When in 2010, the BBC wanted to do a series on the art of bell-ringing, their first port of call was St Peter Mancroft Church. Bells have been rung there more or less continuously since 1431 and Mancroft has consistently been a centre of campanology excellence; in 1715 the Norwich Scholars rang 13 bells changing their order 5,000 times without one repetition.

In the Victorian and early Edwardian period, the background to bell-ringing in St Peter Mancroft was a tragi-comic confrontation between bell-ringers and vicars. Traditionally the former were independent, not always of the parish, and were paid for their services either by churchwardens, private individuals or the Norwich Corporation. They were known to drink as they rang and after they rang, when they adjourned to the White Horse. Their drinking was much frowned upon by the Church and in fact the jug they drank from in the belfry was once confiscated by the vicar. It all came to a head in 1902 when the Reverend *FJ Meyrick*, who wanted all the bell-ringers to be parishioners and to give their services free, locked them out.

No more bells...

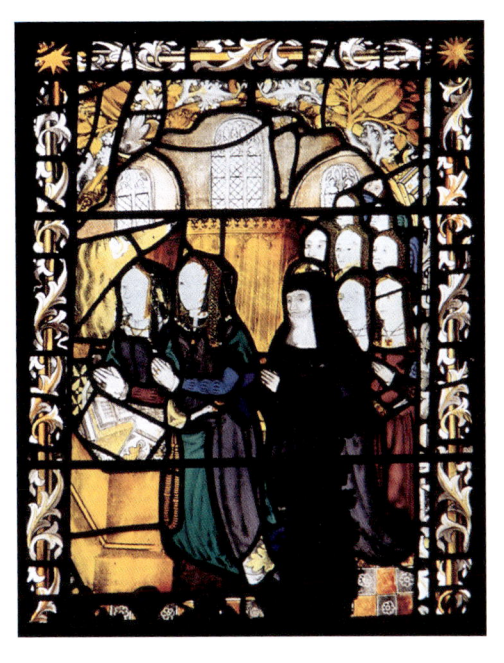

The vicar won and after a period of readjustment all was well again (though the peals from the new ringers were not of the previous high standards). But the bell ringers had not been consulted when changes were made to the floor of the ringing chamber in 1881/82. It had been partly lowered so that the congregation wouldn't see the ringers – and their drinking – during the services. However it meant a six metre drop, hence much longer ropes to pull on and a greater physical effort for the ringers.

The new bell-ringers were led by *Douro Potter* (born 1867) who was also a verger and steeple-keeper. He was the fourth generation of his family to fill this post and had inherited the eccentric streak running through the Potters: the name *Douro*, his son's name *Peter Mancroft*, his idiosyncratic way of dressing with a large hat and other accoutrements – which, people said, made him look like St Peter – and his devotion to the great Norwich writer and natural philosopher Sir Thomas Browne, from whose work he read every evening to his family.

In May 1924 Douro noticed that the bells needed reframing. They were removed and came back a year later. As the bell-ringers tried them for the first time Douro suddenly stopped and collapsed. He died of a heart attack in the bell-ringing chamber which had been part of his life for so long. It was for him that the new bells would toll first.

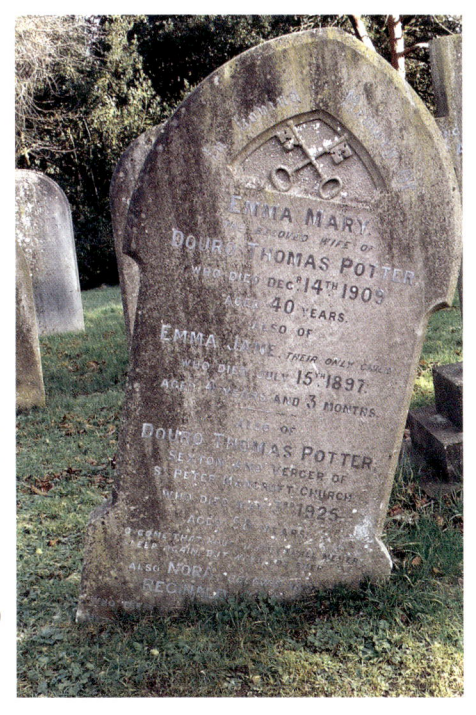

The Caleys

Nathaniel †1867   Albert J. †1895

Napoleon once said disparagingly that the British were a nation of shopkeepers (boutiquiers). He might have been thinking of people like the Caleys. They were the epitome of a successful and enterprising Victorian family of 'shopkeepers' whose creativity wasn't directed towards the arts of warfare so dear to the Corsican general, but to the little luxuries of everyday life.

John Caley and his wife Mary-Ann lived in Windsor and had eight children. Together, in 1823, they established a department store, which made them a household name in Windsor for two centuries. The store closed in 2006.

In those days you expected your daughters to marry and no longer be in your charge, and your sons to join the family business. If a son didn't want to join the family firm and couldn't decently, or profitably, set up in competition, he had to seek his fortune elsewhere.

So it would be that two of the Caleys' sons came to Norwich where they started their own businesses.

The second son Nathaniel was born in 1824 and married Emily Dunn. With an associate Robert Slagg, he established a silk mercer's business but died aged 43 leaving a widow and eight children. Emily remarried and went on to have another family.

The third son, Albert, born in 1829 and married to Elizabeth Bain, is the best known, coming to Norwich in his twenties and opening a chemist shop in London Street. Mineral waters were very fashionable at the time for their medicinal properties; he started producing and selling many different kinds and was so successful that he had to move twice to larger premises. His brother Frederick and son Edward joined the firm and in 1890 they made a final move to Chapelfield where they had their own artesian wells. They were patronised by Royalty and the House of Commons, and exported mineral waters as far as America, Australia and New Zealand.

Caleys started making chocolate in 1886 and this product too was an instant success. They took their cue from Swiss manufacturing techniques and used the best local milk from a herd of Red Poll cattle – a new breed introduced in 1873 – grazing at Whitlingham. They were also quick at reacting to topical events. For example, bars of Marching Chocolate were sent to the front in both World Wars and a special chocolate went on sale in 1953 to mark the Coronation.

Advertisements for their products were well designed, appealing and familiar to all. Some, like the one at the start of this section, were the work of Alfred Munnings, who was employed by them as a graphic designer when he was an apprentice at the printing firm

Page Brothers, and they have remained classics of the genre.

The Caley family appear to have been good employers: it is said that the manufacture of cocoa arose directly from Albert's reluctance to lay off workers when the soft drinks season was over. After his death, Frederick was similarly motivated when he added making crackers to the tasks of women preparing chocolate boxes, thereby lengthening their working year. However, they have been accused of relying heavily on cheap female labour, especially underpaid homeworkers (women who could only work from home and had no bargaining power).

In 1932 Caleys was bought by Mackintosh and Sons. *Nathaniel*'s son *Neville* became a draper like his father, but in Ipswich. At some stage he emigrated to Australia, changed his name to Cayley and his trade to bird painter. His son, Nathaniel's grandson, became a well known Australian ornithologist and bird painter *Neville William Cayley*.

The Caleys' graves are interesting on several counts. It is quite rare for adult siblings to be buried together – it sometimes happened if they hadn't married or moved away – but here we have a large family plot with two brothers, their mother and three nephews, each (except one un-named infant) in a sarcophagus grave of the same design, as if to preserve some sort of unity even in death. What is also unique is that they are lying close to each other, side by side, surrounding their mother/grandmother, thus perhaps replicating an archetypal family gathering.

The very next plot with matching iron railings is occupied by an obelisk on top of a family vault. There lies the *Allen* family, *Elizabeth* and *George* – perhaps others.

It could well be that the *Caleys* and the *Allens* were related. *George* was a glove and cloth weaver like *Nathaniel* and we know they met when the premises in Chapelfield for the Caley factory were passed from *George Allen* to *Albert Caley* in 1880. *George Allen* was not himself averse to taking risks and in 1860 he introduced to Norwich the manufacture of elastic cloth which was a novelty and had only been made in the West of England. Although the facts of this matter have proved elusive, the union of their two families through marriage would have made social and commercial sense and might explain their choice of a resting place.

The rusted railings, the ivy and amber-coloured moss growing on and between the tombs generate an air of faded grandeur and melancholy. More than any other in the cemetery, this resting place, the only tangible relic of the Caleys' earthly empire, is a stark reminder of the certainty of death.

"...the dust returns to the ground it came from..."
(Ecclesiastes 12:7)

Daniel Sayer

†1866

The Horse in the Lecture Theatre.

In the 19th century, in ordinary people's minds, animals could be divided into two groups: horses and the rest. The rest comprised other farm animals: cattle, sheep and pigs which, when sick, could all be attended to by the local healer or cowleech if they were valuable enough.

There were also a few pets, mainly dogs, which were fashionable for those who could afford them but if they sickened there wasn't anyone to turn to. In the 1850s the fashion for stuffing animals was at its peak; small mammals and birds, often shot to order, were sought after to decorate one's drawing room. Should a beloved dog or cat die it could end up at the taxidermist's and then be taken back home where it belonged.

Horses on the other hand, because of their ubiquitous uses, were always in the care of farriers and blacksmiths. These craftsmen could administer the odd traditional remedy but they were ill-equipped to deal with serious diseases and war wounds.

John Sayer was an 'animal and bird preserver' in the early part of the 19th century. His business flourished in a prosperous part of Norwich, St Giles Street, where doctors lived and practised and where medical conferences or meetings took place, usually at the Norfolk Hotel. He had two sons, *Daniel*, born 1815, and *John*, born 1816, who from a young age must have been exposed to animal bodies, skeletons, fur and feathers, on a daily basis. Both boys very likely helped their father in the shop, but only one, John, remained to take over the taxidermy business. Daniel went to London to train as a veterinary surgeon. He was by then in his twenties, relatively late considering he could have gone at 18 or even earlier.

There had been veterinary schools in France and Germany since 1762 and one was established in 1781 in Camden Town (then a rural area to the north of London) by a French refugee, Benoit Vial. Vial modelled it on the one in Alfort, near Paris. The entry requirements were good reading and writing skills and a recommendation! And money for the fees as well, of course.

Although specified to last 18 months, or even three years, the courses at times only lasted a term or so and the student intake, as well as comprising the expected blacksmiths and grooms, was rumoured to also include 'ratcatchers, mutton pie men' and anybody vaguely connected to the animal world to inflate the ranks of fee-paying students. The London college concerned itself nearly exclusively with equine patients; in 1828 the animals admitted to the college infirmary consisted of 869 horses, one ass and 16 dogs.

It took the rinderpest epidemic of the mid-1860s, which decimated thousands of herds of cattle, to awake the nation to the need for veterinary science embracing more than just horses and dogs. When *Daniel Sayer* went up to the veterinary college in 1839 or 1840 the concept of a veterinary surgeon was only just becoming accepted in the public's mind. By 1839 there were just under a thousand vets, graduates of the college, in Britain. The professional foundations of the college were still shaky; in March 1841, the year Daniel graduated, the college was refused a Royal Charter which would have enhanced its status and privileges – something the profession sorely needed. Veterinary surgeons were the butt of endless jokes, cartoons and derogatory comments. As late as 1852 a vet in Spalding, Lincolnshire, R Metherell, had to fight his corner with the following stern notice:

NOTICE!

Mr. FOSTER, *COWLEECH*, issued handbills last week in this market, stating that he had removed from Double-street to Pinchbeck-street, soliciting also a continuance of favors, and designating himself *a Veterinary Surgeon!* Now the term "Veterinary Surgeon" was **a FORGERY**—an appellation to which *he has not the slightest claim.*

To constitute a Veterinary Surgeon, it is essential to be in possession of a **Diploma**, granted by the Court of Examiners of the Royal College of Veterinary Surgeons, London. That, at the said College, Candidates for the said Diploma are taught Anatomy, Physiology, Dissections, and the Nature and Proper Treatment of all Diseases incident to Domesticated Animals, as also Chemistry and Materia Medica; and unless such Candidates are found Proficient in each of these Branches of Veterinary Science on their examination, they are rejected, being considered unqualified to practice.

Mr. FOSTER, like many other **Blacksmiths, Bellhangers, &c.**, professing a knowledge of the **Healing Art**, has not acquired the above essential branches, and consequently will, ere long **be compelled** to represent himself in proper terms, by adopting the words **"FARRIER"** or **"COW-LEECH"** *instead of Veterinary Surgeon.*

The Veterinary Body, under their Royal Charter of Incorporation, have the power of compelling Empirics *to erase from their Door-plates, Sign-boards, &c., the words "Veterinary Surgeon,"* it being an Imposition and a Forgery! and is not allowed by other Professions.

R. METHERELL,
Veterinary Surgeon, and Fellow of the Veterinary Medical Society.

Veterinary Infirmary, Pinchbeck-street, Spalding,
October 18th, 1852.

R. Metherell, who qualified at the College in December 1838, having enrolled in October 1837, attacks a cow-leech for misrepresentation.
(RCVS)

Meanwhile in the 1840s and '50s in Norwich, the Sayer brothers were both established in St Giles Street, each with a large practice. John was preserving and selling all sorts of stuffed animals especially birds, which were in great demand. He was also at the centre of an international trade in birds' eggs. In 1852 he could sell a very rare Willow Wren's egg for three shillings and six pence (that same year an agricultural labourer earned 9s 3½d per week) and an Ortolan Bunting's egg for 1s 6d (1 shilling is worth roughly

£3.73 in today's currency). At his workshop, apart from a secretary, John Goldsmith, to deal with his correspondence, he had apprentices, one of whom, T E Gunn, became arguably the most famous taxidermist of his day. John Sayer and his wife Rebecca only had one child, born to them quite late, and he doesn't seem to have been as prosperous as his brother judging by the fact that they had no live-in servants.

Daniel, one of the county's first qualified vets, had a large practice at 82 St Giles Street. He treated the horses of the well-to-do and no doubt their dogs too.

In 1865 (by which time agricultural wages had risen to 11s 3d per week) *Daniel Sayer* could charge 3s 6d for dressing a wound, and 6s for blistering the sides of a horse. He was also doing a lot of shoeing (two shoes for 2s 6d) which can't have made him very popular with the blacksmiths and farriers whose preserve it had been hitherto. In the 1860s a carpenter in London where (as ever) wages were higher, could expect a maximum of 5s for a day's work – and the social reformer William Booth estimated that, just to get by, an average working family needed 18s to 21s a week. In 1861 *Daniel* and *Maria*'s family included, as well as his four children and three servants, a nephew by the name of *Henry Sayer*, aged 19. Perhaps there was another Sayer brother who died prematurely.

Neither *John* nor *Daniel* lived long enough to fully enjoy their success. They both died in 1866, one aged 51, the other 52. *Daniel* left four orphans, the youngest only five years old, his wife Maria having died aged 37, the previous year. *Daniel* and his wife are buried at Earlham Road, next to several of their relatives. John, who left a ten-year-old daughter, is at the Rosary.

Buried above their station?

De Vear *Last* *Abel*
†1857 †1886 †1883

Along the main drive, in prominent positions near to the chapel, are the most expensive plots. Here one expects to find the great and good of the time. Although in this cemetery there is no ostentatious display of wealth such as the mausolea seen in other Victorian cemeteries, for example Undercliffe, Bradford, and Brookwood, Surrey, there are largish plots with good quality stone monuments, tombs and statues.

Past Lord Mayors, industrialists, sheriffs, surgeons and canons are all represented there. But you also find citizens who left no obvious trace in the world apart from the inscription on their grave, and the fact that they could afford a prime plot as well.

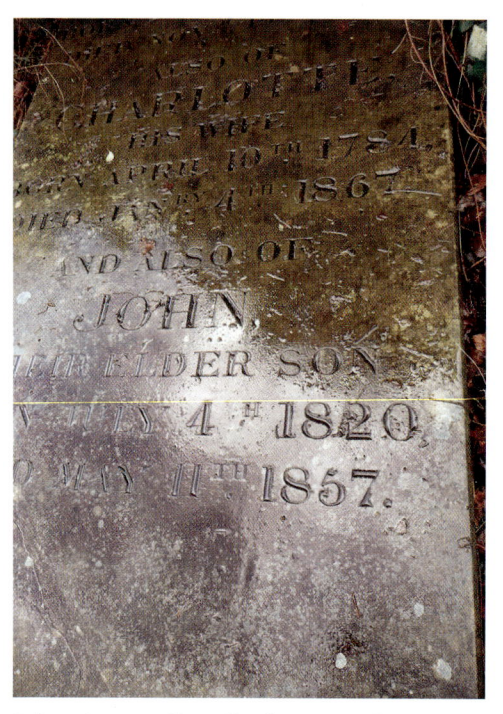

John de Vear and his wife *Charlotte* have a large slab stone, unremarkable except for the carving of the names which is exceptionally large and very carefully done. The stone used, probably marble, is in pristine condition in spite of lying flat on the ground, exposed to the elements for one hundred and fifty years. Their son, *John de Vear junior*, died in 1857, like his father. He is recorded as a warehouse attendant. This humble occupation doesn't match the expensive grave.

The Last family have a low sarcophagus type grave, probably York stone. They were carpenters by trade; again, it is surprising to find them there.

However the de Vear family are named in transactions involving land at Union Street, and number 1 Cow Hill was bought in 1812 by a *John de Vear* for the sum of £220. The de Vear in question described himself as a gentleman, a title which could hide a multitude of sins, and gave his address as the Cathedral Close – a very respectable one. They seemed to have been what we would call nowadays 'property developers'. *John de Vear* junior in 1851, aged 30, was living in London with his wife Rebecca and did not work as such but was in receipt of an annuity. The Lasts had several properties they rented out in the area round Old Post Office Yard, between Bedford Street and Exchange Street. Their wealth, also from property, explains their desire to join those who wanted to be remembered after their death in some style. This wealth is most certainly the cause of *Henry Last's* demise: on Saturday 14th August 1886, a certain *George Harmer* was released from Norwich prison where he had been held for assaulting his wife. He turned up at home in Wild's Yard and on finding that his wife – wisely perhaps – had not stayed to wait for him, he set out obsessively looking for her. After calling at various neighbours and crying he found out that she had gone to her mother's. Without food, money or wife he proceeded to *Henry Last*'s cottage and workshop and killed him. With the money he took from him he ran away to London. *George Harmer* was hanged at Norwich Castle on 13th December 1886, the last person to perish in this way.

The most spectacular monument, along this main drive and even nearer to the chapel, is the white stone statue of a horse. He is not long limbed and elegant like his cousins in equestrian statues, for he is a humble pony. But he is a stallion, his manhood still intact, looking as if he might have come straight from Anderson's meadow. His mane frames his arched neck, his tail is long and curly. He has been immortalised with his head low, despondently pawing the ground, as if mourning. Like his descendants, who still today graze along the Wensum, he is a gypsy pony, perhaps the prize possession of his owner, *John Abel*. We don't know if *John Abel* was particularly attached to this breed or if it was his wife's favourite horse – the memorial was built for her – but interestingly the present day Abel family, well known in Watton, have recently announced their decision to honour their favourite breed, Shire Horses, with a statue in the town (Eastern Daily Press, 16th January, 2013).

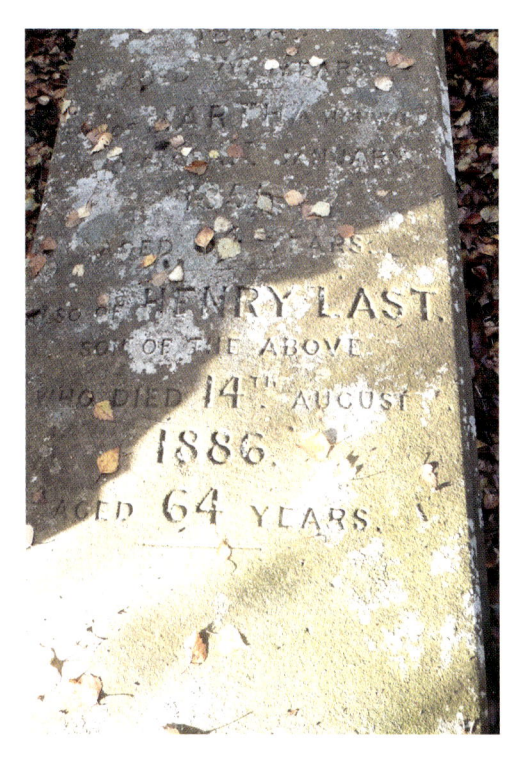

Because of the easy, guaranteed grazing in the Wensum meadows, a number of gypsies settled in Heigham, Costessey and Ringland. John Abel, born in Ringland, was probably of Romany extraction although his family had settled in Norfolk. Apart from buying and selling horses he was also for many years the innkeeper of the Rising Sun on Chapelfied, an occupation which must have offered endless opportunities for interesting business sidelines. His son,

ROADSTER STALLION, THE PROPERTY OF MR. JOHN ABEL, OF NORWICH, 1871.

and later also his grandson helped with the horses and the inn. He was doing so well financially that in 1871 he could afford to commission an engraving of a prized roadster stallion.

By the time he was in his 60s and 70s he had acquired a lot of land and bought a large house with stables and yards in Chapelfied. The house bore the name of a prized race horse he owned called Camperdown, who had won many races for him. *John Abel* described himself throughout his life as a horse dealer but he was obviously much more than that. His will reveals an astute and far seeing businessman who died very wealthy.

The epitaph under his name seems an attempt to stop tongues wagging but it may refer not to his wealth but to the fact that after the death of his first wife, *Frances*, with whom he is buried, *John Abel* married *Eliza* who was thirty nine years younger than him.

Let all the world be silent for God alone is Judge

Ann Mussett
†1904

In mid 19th-century Norwich about 40% of the working population consisted of women, 32% of whom were in domestic service or charring. As the recession of the 1850s took hold, more were to join this number as employment in the manufacturing industries shrank. The Norfolk Chronicle of 5th December 1856 describes the situation: *"Norwich manufacturers may be said to be almost at a standstill. There has not been so complete a state of stagnation for some years past. Hundreds of . . operatives who are usually employed in the production of spring goods are now out of work."*

Ann Mussett was born in 1833. She was from a poor family, probably one of many children and came from Wighton in Norfolk, which was an advantage when looking for a position as employers didn't like their maids to be too streetwise and preferred them to come from the county. Domestic servants like her went into service at an early age, probably ten (or even eight) years old, worked seven days a week from early morning to late at night, except for a break to attend a church service on Sunday morning, and earned no more than their keep to start with.

They could only visit family once a year as they had neither the time nor the money to go more, and over the years, they would often lose touch with them.

Ann stayed with the same employer most of her life (she did marry but was soon widowed). It is reasonable to assume that the family she worked for was fairly humane and treated her well; she would have had no reason to leave.

Their home became her home. Her wages would have gradually crept up to £10-£15 per year and remained in that bracket for the rest of her serving life. She worked as a 'general servant' in the household of *Samuel Critchfield*, a cutler, and his wife *Elizabeth*, who had five grown-up children.

However in 1851, *Samuel Critchfield* was living with a houseful of lodgers whilst his wife and the rest of the family were living with their daughter *Maria*, a schoolmistress. Maria's husband, *Camille Lantenant*, was a French teacher and several of the Critchfield siblings were also teachers. This late family configuration seems to point to reduced circumstances.

When in 1858 the now widowed *Elizabeth Critchfield* died, *Ann Mussett*, who had followed *Elizabeth* and the Critchfield children to the Lantenants, stayed on with them and helped to raise *Samuel* and *Elizabeth's* grandchildren. She was still with them in 1871 and although *Camille* had become a wine agent, the family still didn't seem well off; *Ann* was their only servant. Their lack of means could well be the reason why they didn't keep her on in her old age. We find her, aged 68, in the West Wymer workhouse with about 750 other inmates, a lot of them ex-servants like her. She died there in 1904. Someone in her ex-employers' family must have kept in touch with her and at her death wanted her buried as a family member and not as a pauper.

Ann Mussett is a unique case in this cemetery. A woman like her, who had been in service all her life and wasn't a wife or mother, had no status in the society of the time.

Like all the dispossessed, at her death, she would normally have disappeared into a common grave and oblivion. But, touchingly, she was buried in the same grave as her first mistress, *Elizabeth,* and thus preserved in our memory on an equal footing.

In
Memory of
ELIZABETH ANN,
WIFE OF THE LATE
SAMUEL CRITCHFIELD
WHO DIED 3RD MAY 1858.
BLESSED ARE THE DEAD WHICH DIE IN THE LORD
REV XIV 13
ALSO OF
ANN MUSSETT,
AN OLD SERVANT OF THE FAMILY
WHO DIED 11TH APRIL 1904,
AGED 71 YEARS.

Amenaide Vulliamy

†1902

Most people settling in a foreign country – whatever the reason – will generally want to blend in and not cause cultural or linguistic embarrassment to their hosts. Hence the simplification and anglicization of the names they brought with them, for example: Révère became Revere, Peñãluna/Penaluna, Gonçalves/Goncalves, even Becquette/Beckett. All these names have been recorded in Norwich.

Amenaide Helene Vulliamy was born Amenaïde Hélène de Champlouis in 1845, in Switzerland, into a minor branch of an old French aristocratic family, which included diplomats, top civil servants, members of the judiciary, inventors and an early photographer, Victor Nau de Champlouis.

As was the norm at that time for the offspring of the bourgeoisie and the aristocracy, *Amenaide* probably had an arranged marriage to *Theodore Vulliamy*, a clock-maker. He was descended from a famous Swiss clock-making family who had settled in London in 1730 and the family was wealthy. The Vulliamy clocks were of such quality that the diplomatic mission in Peking presented one to the Emperor in 1793. They are still very sought after. One for sale at the time of writing (April 2013) is expected to fetch between £150,000 and £250,000. The only known local one is in the clock tower at Somerleyton Hall. (Note 5).

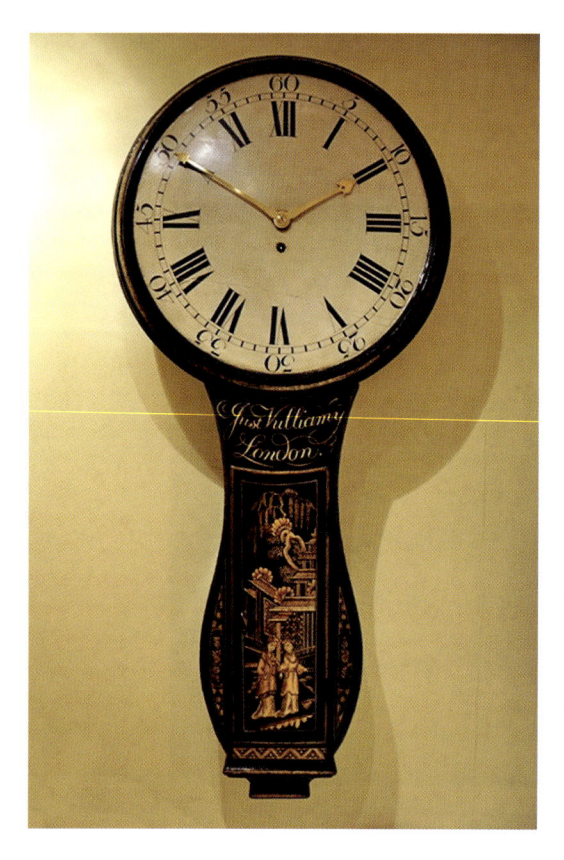

Amenaide and *Theodore* settled in France where their five children (Marie Elizabeth, Alice, Herbert, Justin and Edward) were born. The only record of their life at that time is a legal one: the formal break up of a business partnership in Normandy involving Theodore and two associates. The family resurfaced in England in 1881 when Alice (16) and Justin (11) (Note 6) were living in Eastbourne with their aunt, Elizabeth Vulliamy. Theodore had a new family in Ware, Hertfordshire, although he never divorced nor remarried. There was no trace of Amenaide. Could she have gone back to Switzerland or France?

It takes her death, more than 20 years later, on 4th February 1902, to reveal why she was buried in Norwich where she had no obvious connection: she was an inmate of Heigham Hall, the last privately owned 'lunatic asylum' in the country. Her epitaph hints at the sadness of her life.

The darkness is past and the true light now shineth
(1 John 11:8)

In spite of her large family, she is marooned in a foreign cemetery, alone in her grave, which is nowadays concealed under a very ancient and wild bramble bush.

HEIGHAM HALL NEAR NORWICH.

AMENAIDE HELENE VULLIAMY,
WIFE OF THEODORE VULLIAMY,
DIED 4TH FEBRUARY 1902,
AGED 57 YEARS.
"THE DARKNESS IS PAST AND THE TRUE LIGHT
NOW SHINETH" I. JOHN II. 8

The Greens and the Markwells

†1880 to 1886

In the 19th and early 20th century in Europe and America, childbirth was a risky enterprise. It was the main cause of women's deaths, in the form of puerperal fever and birth complications. So much so that churches said special prayers for women who had given birth, thanking God for *"safe deliverance and preservation from the dangers of childbirth"*.

A small number of physicians on both sides of the Atlantic became convinced that their colleagues were responsible for the high maternal mortality rate due to their lack of hygiene.

In some hospitals doctors would go straight from a dissection to assisting a birth without realising the need to wash their hands. Most women knew that giving birth in hospital could be a death sentence and many waited too long on purpose, hoping to give birth before reaching the hospital. A physician of the time found that death rates were much lower in 'street births' than in hospital births. Whistleblowers, themselves often physicians and scientists, who pointed at doctors' lethal practices were ridiculed and hounded. The most memorable example is that of Ignaz Semmelweis, professor of medicine in Vienna, who introduced hand-washing in 1847, thus notably reducing the incidence of puerperal fever. He was dismissed, harassed and put in an asylum where, severely beaten by the wardens, he died of septicaemia a fortnight later. It took Pasteur's discoveries on the bacterial causes of puerperal fever in 1879 to shift medical opinion, although it was not until 1929 that masks and rubber gloves were made mandatory in this country for each delivery.

Norwich was a dangerous place in which to live. *The Lancet* noted that, of 20 larger towns dealt with by the Registrar-General during the period 1870 to 1878, Norwich had the highest mortality rate. Also, in spite of the fact that a network of sewers had been established in 1870 in an effort to reduce the occurrence of such events, there were scarlet fever and typhus epidemics in the city. Smallpox and cholera were never far away although generally in the whole country mortality rates dropped from the 1870s onwards. All over Europe inner city areas had high rates of tuberculosis but by the 1880s the disease had peaked and was steadily declining.

When *James Green*, an assistant to a pawnbroker married *Eliza* in July 1878, she was 18 years old. In November 1880, she died aged 20. A year later in October 1881, James remarried. His bride *Elizabeth* was 19 years old. In July 1882, she died aged 20, nine months after her wedding. In February 1886, four years after his second wife, *James* died aged 26, of tuberculosis.

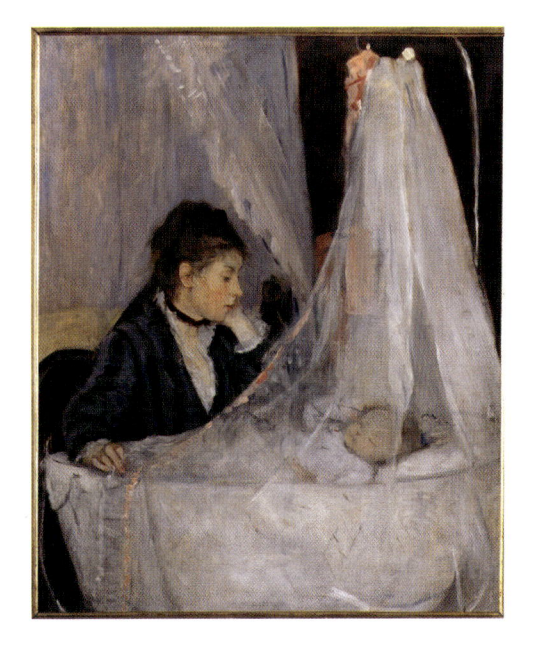

In 2009 the infant mortality rate in Norwich was 7.5 per 1,000 births and although it is the highest in the East of England (Norfolk NHS statistics), the figure looks very small compared to 200-300 per 1,000 births recorded in 18th-century England or even the 150 per 1,000 it had dropped to by the 1840s. The most common afflictions killing young children were measles, scarlet fever, diarrhoea and diphtheria. In England in 1883 there was yet another measles epidemic.

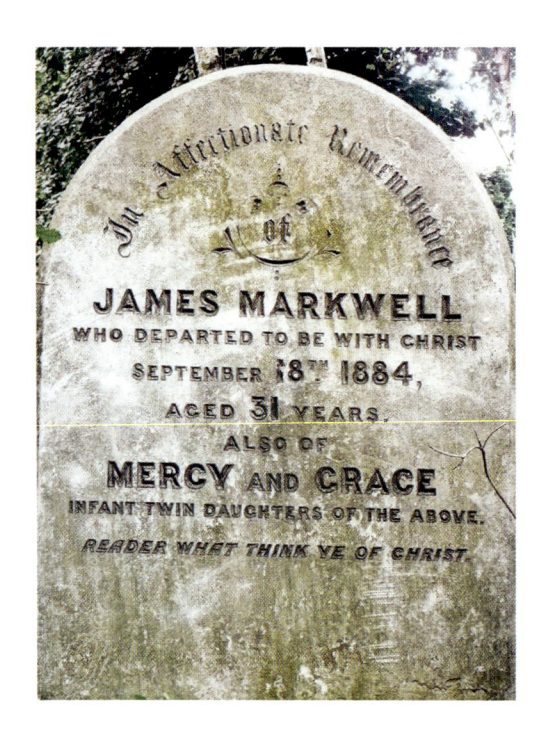

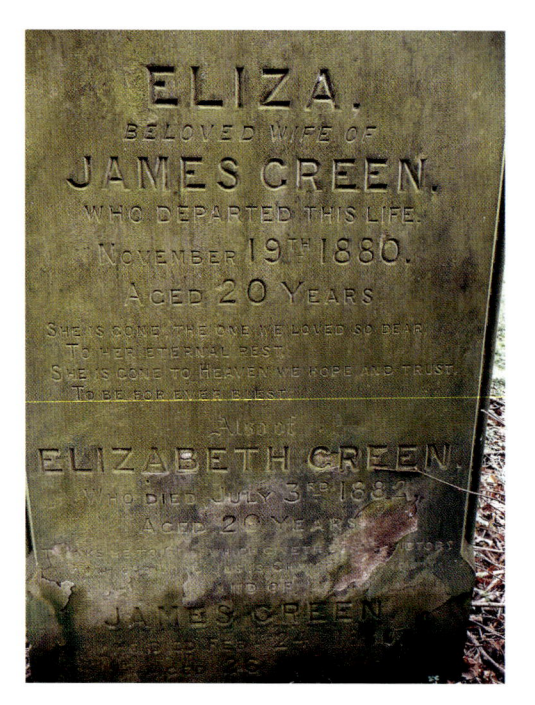

When *James* and *Maria Markwell's* twins were born in 1882, the names they were given point to a possible long wait for their arrival: they were called *Mercy* and *Grace*. Sadly, they died in their first year in August 1883. *James*, their father, aged 31, who was a grocer's assistant, died after a short and painful illness in September 1884. The family lived in Oxford Street, Parish of St Peter Mancroft, very close to the Norfolk and Norwich hospital which had been established in 1770. *James* and the twins are buried together. *Maria*, having lost all her family, chose an epitaph for their grave which is an expression of bitterness and revolt seldom recorded on a grave stone:

Reader what think ye of Christ.

George Skipper
†1948

The architect *George Skipper* is someone to whom the people of Norwich owe a great debt. He played a big part in making the city visually attractive and not just functional; he is one of those few architects who managed not to make us regret the buildings that used to stand there as he replaced them by beautiful original new ones. Quite a feat! There are about ten landmark buildings designed by him between 1896 and 1923 which, like the Royal Arcade or Jarrolds are there for all to admire and enjoy at any time.

However his trademark details are only revealed to the scrutiny of the curious: panels and friezes reminiscent of medieval art, windows and gables inspired from Renaissance architecture, tracery and motifs from Art Nouveau, turrets, domes and chimney stacks adorning his roofs, facades with columns aplenty and sometimes deliberately asymmetrical. His exotic and exuberant spirit has echoes of the great Catalan Antoni Gaudí, his close contemporary. Skipper could also do grand, baroque buildings like Surrey House in Surrey Street and the Norwich and London Insurance Association's offices in St Giles Street.

He embraced a wide range of materials from terracotta (Cosseyworks) to marble of various kinds from Italy, ceramics, stone and brick. "Il fait feu de tout bois" (he makes a fire with any wood), as the French would say.

His creations are a blend of styles from different epochs and cultures but what they have in common is that they all exude *joie de vivre*. There is no hint of understatement or austerity in his work which spanned three quarters of a century. He died at 93, survived by his third wife, who was much younger than him. He is buried with his first wife.

In the cemetery, behind the burial chapel, there is a smallish, unprepossessing gravestone of a dull colour, stained by black lichen, with straight corners and poor lettering which will soon be completely unreadable. There is no decoration of any sort, no sign of care or love. And there, sadly, lie the remains of this visionary architect who left us a unique legacy.

George Skipper was a member of the Plymouth Brethren.

Rosetta Soman
†1877

HAPPY OLD AGE.

Rosetta Salomon was born in 1801 in Whitechapel, London. Little did she know that she was to become the matriarch of a very large family, successful socially, economically and politically.
She married *David Soman* who was a French Jew, born in Whitechapel in 1796. His parents had emigrated to England from Luneville, Lorraine, in the last years of the 18th century. Ironically, this was just when the life of Jews in France was about to take a turn for the better, thanks to the French Revolution of 1789, starting with the abolition of a crippling tax on Jewish businesses. It was probably this tax which had driven David Soman's parents to leave France.

David converted his first fur cap-making business into one of the earliest Norwich boot- and shoe-making firms in Surrey Mews. He was a successful businessman, active in the community at large and in the Jewish congregation.

Meanwhile Rosetta gave birth to nine children, most of whom stayed in the shoe trade.

When her daughter Rachel married Phillip Haldinstein, a Prussian Jew, in Norwich in 1846, he took over the shoe business and greatly expanded it, renaming it Haldinstein and Sons. The reputation of the firm was such that they were entrusted with making the bridal shoes for Mary, Princess Royal, daughter of King George V and Queen Mary, when she married Henry Lascelles, 6th Earl of Harewood, in 1922.

In the 1880s and 1890s, however, it seems that the Haldinsteins were far from good employers. They paid the lowest rates locally and deducted 'grindery', that is, the cost of heating, lighting and work space, from the wages of those working on site. This kind of exploitation is what drove the membership growth of the trade union movement at that time. Norwich was known as a place where wages were low. The radical magazine *Daylight* reported on 14th July 1890 that *"for a long while the Executive at Union HQ have felt that something must be done to place Norwich workmen on an equal footing with other towns"*. (Note 7).

Rosetta's son Philip, a printer, became involved with newspaper publishing and in 1863 founded the *Norwich Argus*, which remained in existence till 1892.

Her daughter-in-law, *Philip Soman*'s wife, had eleven children, four of whom died in infancy.

The shoe business, which by then had branches outside Norwich, employed about 2,000 people at the time that it was sold by Rosetta's descendants to the Swiss firm Bally in 1933.

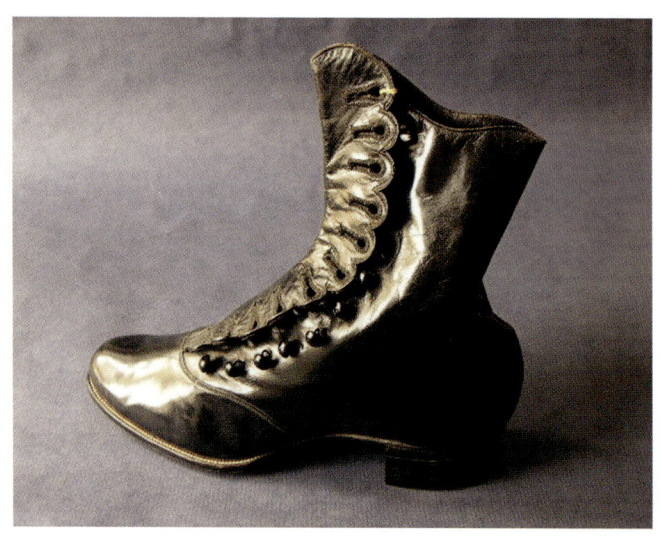

Rosetta's great-grandson *Arthur Michael Samuel* became Financial Secretary to the Treasury in the government of Stanley Baldwin, the Lord Mayor of Norwich, its first Jewish Mayor and the first Lord Mancroft. He was a polymath who wrote essays on a wide variety of topics, from finance to ladies' fans! He published a book on herring fisheries and another on the artist Piranesi.

His daughter *Victoria Mancroft*, born in 1952, married Prince Frederick of Prussia, whose father was Kaiser Wilhelm. If the latter hadn't abdicated, Victoria would have been the wife of the German Emperor and King of Prussia. This was a great social rise which Rosetta, long buried in 1877, would have appreciated.

Her grave in the Jewish cemetery stands surrounded by most of her extended family: the *Somans*, the *Haldinsteins* and the *Samuels*, from babes in arms, to men who left their mark on the city and the nation, all buried within feet of one another.

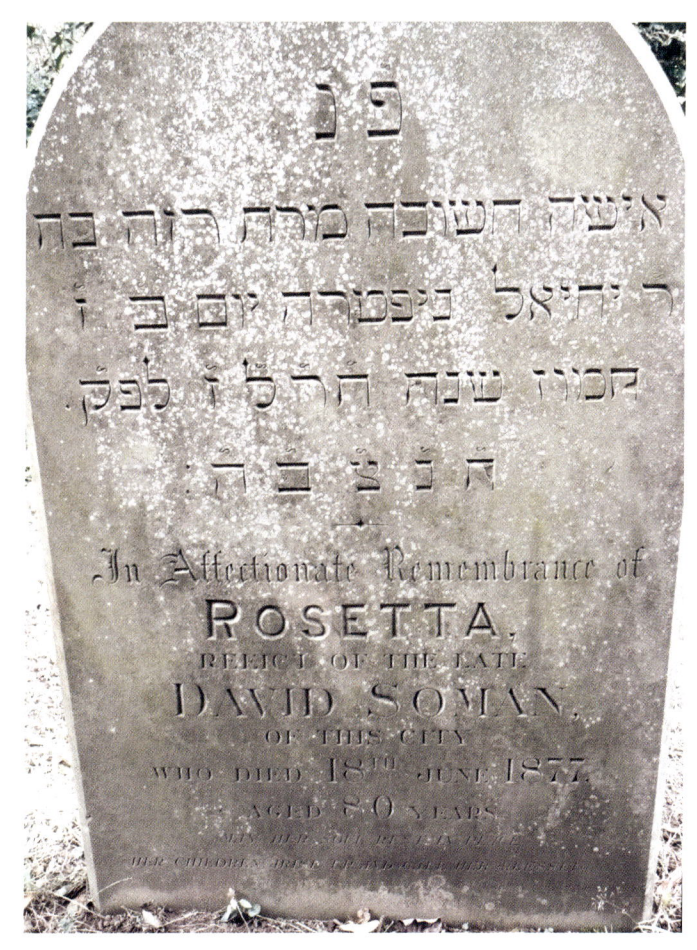

Sarah Rice
†1907

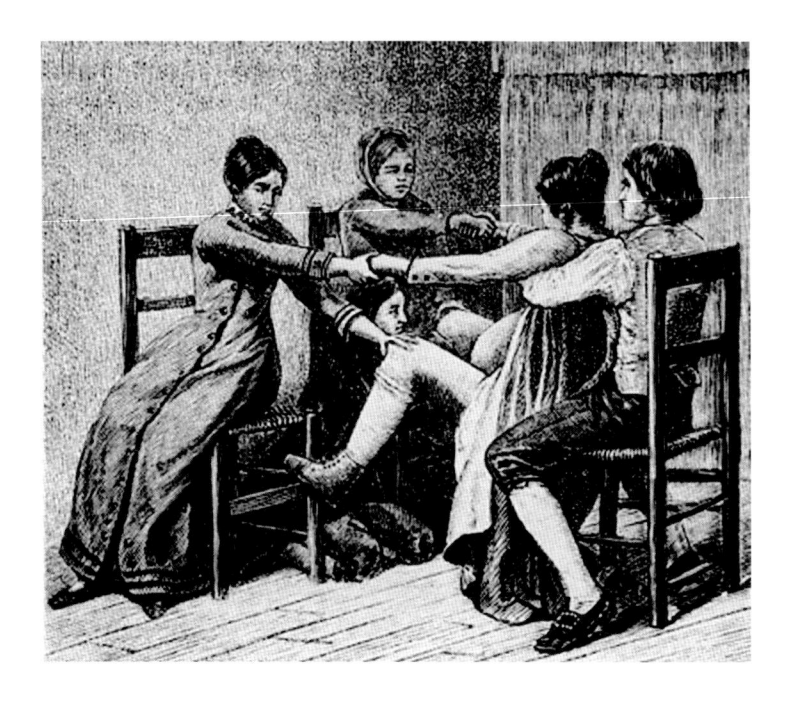

Male gravestones often record their owner's trade or occupation (see page 12) but there is only one grave in the cemetery from Victorian and Edwardian times to record a woman's occupation. *Sarah Rice* who died in 1907, aged 67, was a midwife. Women have been midwives since time immemorial and with experience could do a good job. In Britain, in medieval times the Church even allowed them to christen babies they judged about to die (they also had to report suspicious family happenings!) but in the 16th century male surgeons started to appropriate the lucrative end of this field of activity i.e., the confinement of well-to-do women. The Church stopped supporting them. So middle-class, educated women were no longer attracted to the profession. When only women too poor to pay were left as clients, they couldn't make a living from it.

Sarah Rice was born *Sarah Softley*, in 1840. By then surgeons were demanding the prohibition of midwives on the grounds of 'incompetence'. A campaign against women midwives was launched, with *The Lancet* at its head, writing in 1842: *"the women of England are... wholly deficient both in the moral and physical organisation necessary for performing the duties of that most responsible office"*. (Note 8). Well, of course by then only poor uneducated women often living in squalor like their charges were left to practise. They were often paid in kind (a few eggs or vegetables). Sarah couldn't have trained formally as it was a fee-paying course and she was from a humble background. She probably learned through practice, perhaps helping a more mature midwife like her mother on her rounds. Whatever the case, she had to work as she was widowed in her thirties and needed to support herself and her son, *Raymond*. She was helped in that she was able to live with her nephew *George Softley* who was a coal-carter and a conspicuous character, well known in the community not to suffer fools gladly, and his family.

By 1881 the situation of midwifery was so dire, with women unable to practise on the whole range of confinements (and male practitioners experimenting with novel methods, some good, some not so good – being reprimanded officially for using scissors and knives to cut out wombs and intestines!) that three educated midwives started a counter campaign.

With the support of a rich philanthropist, Louisa Hubbard, they founded the Matrons' Aid, a forerunner of the Royal College of Midwives. But it wasn't until 1902 when Sarah was about to retire that a Midwives Act put paid to the male assault on the profession – albeit not enough to prevent the most lucrative part of the work staying in male hands. When Raymond, who became a carpenter, reached adulthood Sarah lived with him and his family and on census forms she describes herself as head of the family, with other family members defined in relation to her as son, daughter-in-law and grandchildren. This is unusual and befits a strong and independent woman used to making life and death decisions on an everyday basis.

So, although there is no information to this effect, it is likely that Sarah Rice practised midwifery all her adult life in the poorer districts of Norwich, perhaps even servicing a workhouse like the one in West Wymer, Heigham, where the West Norwich Hospital now stands, near where she lived in Tinkler's Lane (now Midland Road).

Sarah's family could rightly be proud of her.

She is buried in unconsecrated ground which may indicate that, like the Softleys mentioned above, she was a Salvationist. (Note 9).

Kiyoshi Hata

†1903

In the 19th or early 20th century, before cinema and television, circuses were the most common form of public entertainment after the music hall. Their repertoire encompassed a wide variety of acts featuring trick-riding, trapeze and high-wire artistes, acrobats, dancers, musicians, clowns and exotic animals, sometimes hundreds of them.

Hamburg was the largest exotic animal market in Europe. In the 1880s and 1890s a trader by the name of Karl Hagenbeck captured the animals in Africa, particularly Somalia, and they were shipped across the Red Sea. Then they were tamed by M. Mellerman, Hagenbeck's brother-in-law and sold ready to be trained to circuses all over Europe. The circuses travelled to their public and toured not only Britain and Europe but America and even Australia and the Far East.

In 1899 Barnum and Bailey's circus came to Norwich and needed four trains to transport their menagerie. A photo of that time shows some of the 21 elephants parading along Prince of Wales Road, along with 70 horses! They set up at Dix's Land, off Unthank Road.

At the beginning of the 20th century Italian and Japanese artistes were particularly sought after so in 1903 George Gilbert, proprietor of the Gilbert circus, engaged a troupe of Japanese acrobats for three weeks for a forthcoming tour. They were to perform in Norwich at the Agricultural Hall, which had been opened in 1882 precisely for circuses, exhibitions and later silent film shows.

One of the artistes was twelve years old, Kiyoshi Hata, who sadly never had a chance to perform. He fell ill with what Dr Burton-Fanning, in charge of the case at the time, called 'brain fever' (meningitis) in the first week of their stay and died on 14th March 1903. The few facts of his short life carved in the stone are particularly intriguing and poignant.

Casualities of war

At the beginning of the 20th century *Ann* and *Clement Holland* lived in Patterson Road and were bringing up their three children. Their second son, *Arthur*, was called up in the First World War and killed in action in April 1918. He is buried at Passchendaele. *Clement*, probably grief-stricken, followed his son to the grave in February 1921. *Ann*, having lost half her family, was still living in Patterson Road when the Second World War broke out. During the last week of April 1942, both her children were with her: her daughter *Sarah* who lived with her and her son *Patrick*, a moulder and core-maker, who was just visiting. During the night of the 27th, at the beginning of the so-called Baedeker raids, a bomb fell on Patterson Road, annihilating what was left of this family. Thus all of them died at the hands of the same enemy.

Arthur Holland †April 1918
Clement Holland †February 2nd 1921
Ann Holland †April 27th 1942
Patrick Holland ditto
Sarah Monaghan ditto

Not far from this grave is that of five men who also died on 27th April 1942, during the same raids. All were employed by Norwich Corporation and were single men, living in lodgings, two in Bacton Road and three at 55 Livingstone Street. The latter were in fact lodging with their former boss, *Henry Barber*, who had recently retired as a foreman for the Norwich Corporation, and his wife *Eliza* and son *Alfred*, a master baker.

One of the bombs fell on nearby Northumberland Street, killing several people and destroying many buildings in that street.

The force of the blast was such that the six inhabitants of 55 Livingstone Street were killed and blown out of the windows by the shockwaves. They were the only casualties on the street. The house still stands intact.

Alfred Barber 28/04/1942 aged 32
Eliza Barber 28/04/1942 aged 64
Henry Barber 28/04/1942 aged 67
James Clarke 30/04/1942 aged 55
Joseph Delamere 27/04/1942 aged 46
Laurence Gaffney 30/04/1942 aged 47

Altogether the Baedeker raids took 254 lives in Norwich alone and destroyed thousands of buildings including seven medieval churches; they were of no strategic benefit to Hitler's forces, just an exercise in reprisals for the Allied Forces' bombing of Lübeck.

Not far from the Norwich Corporation and the Holland graves is the newer of two war cemeteries contained within the general cemetery. Great care was taken in the design of war cemeteries and the best architects and horticulturalists such as Edwin Lutyens and Gertrude Jekyll were involved. This small inner cemetery is enclosed by a thick, low hedge and a metal gate leads you into a different world.

It is a solemn place, but not a sombre one, where the initial sadness is tempered by the harmonious effect of rows of identical white stones, each with a small rose bush, on a background of fresh green turf, lovingly tended and nurtured.

In this intimate resting place lie the fallen of both World Wars and Allied combatants of many countries. A great variety of regimental badges are carved on the white stones, including two whole rows of imperial eagles for the Polish forces.

And at the foot of a much taller, dark green hedge, right at the back, as if hiding, is a row of graves with the cross of the German Empire. In one of those graves lie the remains of four Luftwaffe airmen, who flew from Holland to drop their bombs on Norwich on 9th May 1942. Harassed by the anti-aircraft fire, their Dornier 217 hit a balloon cable, set up to damage enemy planes, over Lakenham. It was then shot down over Stoke Holy Cross and finally crashed at West Green farm, Poringland. These four German airmen are buried amongst the people they were sent to kill: allowed, in death, to rejoin the family of man.

W. Böllert † 9th May 1942
R. Bucksch † 9th May 1942
A. Otterbach † 9th May 1942
M. Speuser † 9th May 1942

Henry Firth

† 1918

Henry W Firth, born in 1888, was the eldest child of a large family living in Sprowston Road. Out of eight children born to *Henry* and *Harriet Firth*, his parents, only four survived into adulthood. His father was a boot and shoe worker and the family was poor. So Henry left school early and went to work in the shoe industry like his father, followed by all his siblings one after the other. In the 1860's, 70's and 80's the shoe trade was experiencing a period of expansion. However the wages were kept low; as late as 1886 women's wages hovered around three shillings per week, men's didn't rise above twelve shillings, so everyone in the Firth family needed to be in work. When the First World War broke out, having repeatedly refused to serve and possibly kill, he was twice sentenced to a year in prison as a conscientious objector. At the end of his second year in Maidstone prison, without being examined by a doctor, he was sent to work at Princetown settlement (part of Dartmoor Prison).

A fellow CO describes what followed: *"broken in health both physically and mentally by long imprisonment, he was sent to work here on the bleak moors, at a time when the weather was at its worst and in spite of the fact that from the first he appeared to be in a dying condition. He was ordered to the Heavy Quarry Party; the change from confinement in a prison to the high bleak hills of Dartmoor was so sudden that the poor fellow suffered terribly from the cold and when too weak to work was charged with slacking. A number of times he endeavoured to get treatment at the hospital but was turned down with a sneer and a gibe about the "men in the trenches". His comrades here did their best, purchasing nourishing and appetising food from the village, but he was broken beyond recovery and fast wasted away. He was admitted into hospital after the glaring, callous negligence of the authorities had roused the temper of the camp. We wired for his wife, they had not seen each other for a whole year, but he died before she arrived."* (Note 10).

His farewell procession from Dartmoor was of huge symbolic significance; a male voice choir started the cortege, followed by hundreds of men who walked four abreast through the prison gates and into the mist of the moors. Behind them was Henry's coffin carried by the Norwich CO contingent. The funeral cortege went through the town which was shrouded in mist with only one or two houses having bothered to draw their curtains as a mark of respect.

They arrived at the railway station with the choir singing

> *"So long thy power hath blessed me*
> *Sure it still will lead me on"*

and just as the doors of the little train were being closed, the last verse rang out and Henry Firth's coffin left for Norwich.

Two days later, 543 conscientious objectors withdrew their labour for a day in protest of the treatment of COs by doctors and wardens.

At the inquest the solicitor acting on behalf of his widow, Ethel, asked questions with the object of showing that Firth was not treated as he should have been. However Dr Battiscombe and Dr Hillyer both stated that every attention was given.

The jury returned a verdict of 'death from natural causes' and announced that they considered that the man had received proper attention. This verdict can be seen as a reflection of the bellicose national mood and the public vilification of COs.

Joshua Pearce

†1904

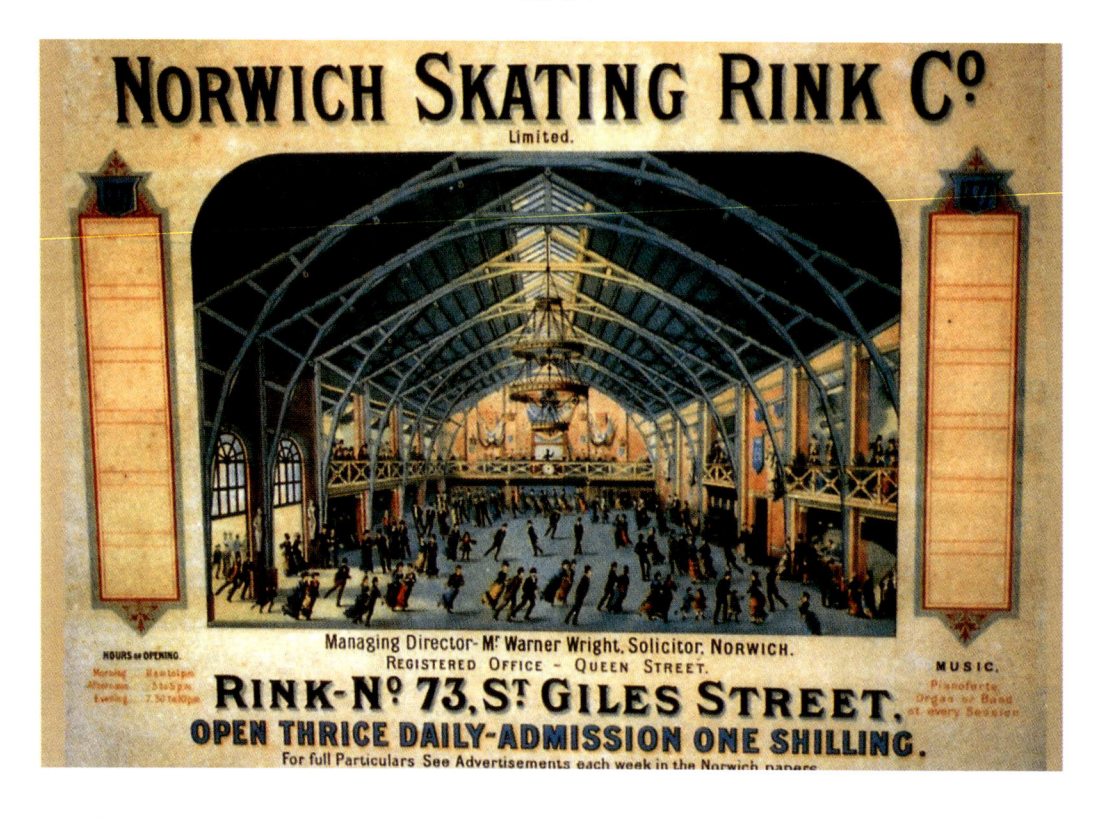

The Salvation Army, founded in the East End of London by William Booth in 1865, became established in Norwich in August 1882. They rented The Old Skating Rink, which could then be accessed through St Giles Street, as the craze for skating had subsided and the building was redundant. However by 1891 the building was in such a bad state of repair, with water pouring in, and the congregation having to open umbrellas to keep dry, that it was decided to buy another St Giles Street site and develop it.

This site was where a cycle-maker had been established after the introduction of velocipedes to Norwich from France in 1869. The cycle factory closed because, annoyed by noise and pollution, the residents had gathered a petition. When they learned that the site had been purchased by the Salvation Army they were equally horrified and raised another petition.

This was understandable. St Giles Street was a desirable address and the Salvation Army was attracting people who were not decorous and who would then be seen loitering in the street, thus lowering the tone of their neighbourhood. However, the construction of the new building, designed by architect Gilbert Scott, went ahead and it was opened on Sunday 30th October 1892.

When they were first established, in the 1880s and '90s, Salvation Army members were often attacked in public. They were teetotallers and temperance campaigners who targeted alcoholics and people whose drinking was their relief from poverty, as well as prostitutes and beggars. Publicans, fast losing trade through the conversions, paid a retinue of people willing to throw rocks, rats and other projectiles at Salvation Army personnel and generally assaulting them. They really needed to be an army!

Contemporary Salvationist, J Mann, kept a diary:

> Black eyes &c were a common occurrence, not that a black eye is very serious, it was the stones which was by far the most dangerous. without a doubt many will carry the marks received by missiles &c to their graves. Once in particular we were marching along, stones were being thrown from a distance in front of us, a coal cart came along, the man was as black as a sweep, he got out of his cart and gave some of them such a horse whipping they must have remembered it for days afterwards, this man for many years was Sergeant Major of the Corps, namely Sergeant Major Softley, this was the first time that he particularly came under my notice, and it shew him to be a fighter anyway.

Joshua Pearce was an early member of the Norwich branch and did not escape unscathed. Reynolds Newspapers of the 15th October 1882 reported:

"On Monday at the Norwich Police-court, Alfred Kindred, of the Star Hotel, Haymarket, Norwich, was charged with unlawfully assaulting Joshua Pearce, a member of the Salvation Army. The complainant stated that on Sunday evening, about seven o'clock, he was going to the Skating Rink in St. Giles, Norwich, now the barracks of the Salvation Army, when he was accosted by the defendant, who struck him on the chest, calling out, "This is the man", or "You are the man that struck me." The magistrates expressed their opinion that the charge against Kindred had been established, and that he had acted disgracefully, interrupting people going to the Skating Rink. The defendant said he had not interfered with any one. The chairman of the bench said the magistrates thought otherwise, and they accordingly fined him £2, and 7s.6d. costs."

Joshua and his wife *Sarah*, born and brought up around Horsham St Faith, married and raised their own family there. In 1861 both they and their eldest daughter, Emma (16) were working as agricultural labourers. They had three younger children, Emily (8), Alfred (5), and Thurza (3). Within the next ten years Joshua and Sarah moved to Heigham and all the children left home, even Thurza, who before the age of 13, went into service in Gladstone Street, Norwich (Heigham). At that time, Joshua was found working as a carter in an ironworks, then as a grocer's carter. In 1891 a labourer in Norwich earned 3 1/2d an hour i.e. just under three shillings for a ten hour day. Joshua Pearce wouldn't have earned any more.

By the late 1890s the Salvation Army, seen to work tirelessly for the poor and destitute, had grown steadily and spectacularly and added an insurance arm to their charitable activities. So Joshua, being a trusted member and the treasurer of the branch, finished his days as an insurance agent, employed by the Army. In 1902 the Sunday congregation averaged 2,128 (much more in winter when life was harder) and had about 570 'soldiers' and 'recruits' on the roll.

Joshua was a very popular and active member of the Army. As an

'Uncle Josh' Pierce, first treasurer

elder he had a public role, leading pageants, opening ceremonies and ministering to the poor. He was held in great affection by those who knew him. Every one called him 'Uncle Josh' and older members of the Army even today remember their parents and grandparents talking about Uncle Josh.

He died in 1904 aged 74 and his grave proudly displays the Salvation Army crest as its only decoration and his nickname *Uncle Josh*. (Note 11).
His wife died in 1923 and is buried with him.

Man proposes, God disposes

Eliza Stevenson

†1862

On 17th July 1862 *Eliza Stevenson*, aged 29, wife of *Henry Stevenson*, one of the proprietors of the *Norfolk Chronicle*, of Upper Surrey Street, was in a phaeton going in the direction of All Saints Church. The horse started off at full speed, the phaeton was upset and Mrs Stevenson sustained fatal injuries and died within the hour. She is buried with one of her children who had died the previous year. *Henry* remarried but sadly his second wife, *Emilia*, also died at 29. She is buried in the same grave with some of *her* children.

Mary Ann Taylor
†1874

The railway line from Norwich to Yarmouth was one of the first to be installed, in 1844. Taking the train in 1874 was still a bit of an adventure and as a lot of people couldn't afford it, it was a glamorous thing to do. It wasn't free of risk though and train crashes were relatively frequent.

In August 1863 on the newly-opened line between King's Lynn and Hunstanton a derailment, caused by a bullock straying on the line, killed five people. On 10th September 1874 *Mary Ann Taylor*, a 47-year-old woman, living in Blofield with her husband George, took an evening train to return home after a day in Norwich, possibly visiting one of her two married children. Her train to Yarmouth collided head on with one from Yarmouth, between Norwich Station and Brundall, on a single track stretch of the line.

Both trains were running late, and were going at full speed to make time, but due to an error by the telegraph clerk, both drivers received authority to proceed. The accident killed the two drivers, two firemen and 21 passengers leaving 75 seriously injured. Some of the victims were buried at the Rosary cemetery but Mary Ann Taylor joined her parents-in-law who were already buried in Earlham Road.

This remains the most serious head-on collision in the history of railways in Britain.

Albert Forster

†1895

The year 1895 was a landmark for imperial China; it had been defeated by the Japanese and on 17th April it signed a humiliating treaty relinquishing Korea and some other provinces.

As well as being engaged in an actual war with Japan, the Chinese Emperor had been besieged for years by foreign companies wanting to build railways.

The first railway line, the Woosung Road Railway, was built by the British-founded firm Jardine Matheson, but was promptly dismantled and sold to Taiwan as it had been built without the consent of the Emperor. Shanghai and its river the Woosung were the epicentre of foreign activity, European powers with bases there vying for influence and new markets.

On 11th April 1895 an explosion at a fort on the banks of the river killed 50 Chinese soldiers. That same day *AJ Forster*, who most likely was working for a British firm in the area, is recorded as having drowned in the Woosung.

We shall never know the true cause of his death, or if drowning was just what the family was told. It is difficult to know what really happened in a foreign country at troubled times.

Wladzilaw Slizewski and Eugenia Zagajewska
†1946

After the end of WW2 thousands of Polish forces personnel were still in Europe, partly on military duty, partly to delay going back to Poland with the communists now in charge. In Britain alone there were about 200,000 Poles. *Wladzilaw Slizewski* was a student at the Polish Naval College near Stirling and his fiancée, *Eugenia Zagajewska* was in the Polish WAAF. They came to spend the Easter weekend in Norfolk and on 22nd April 1946, Easter Monday, they went to Buxton to do some canoeing. The canoe they boarded was a makeshift contraption built with the discarded auxiliary petrol tank of a plane. Wladzilaw had used it twice before on his own. But with two of them the canoe became unstable, capsized and sank. According to eye-witnesses, Eugenia, terrified, clung to Wladzilaw so tightly that he could not save her nor himself. Having survived the war, they drowned in the Bure in six feet of water. They were 21 years old.

They are buried side by side in the military cemetery.

68

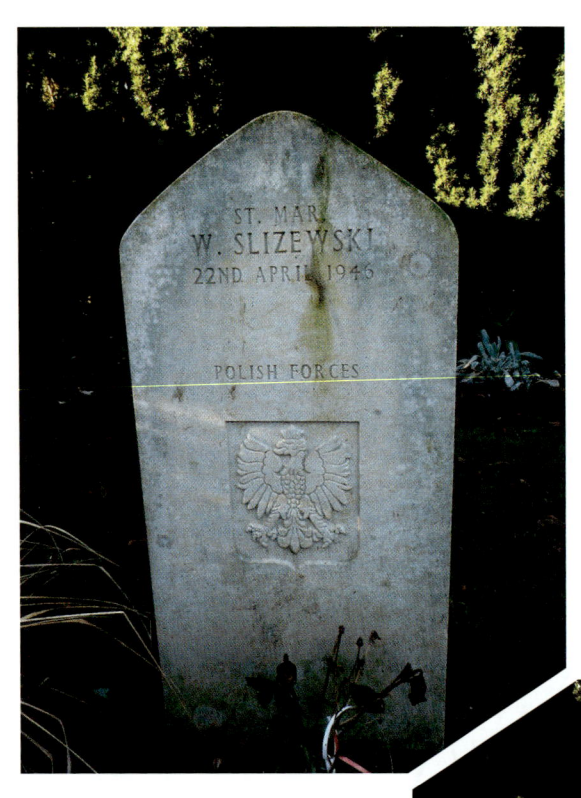

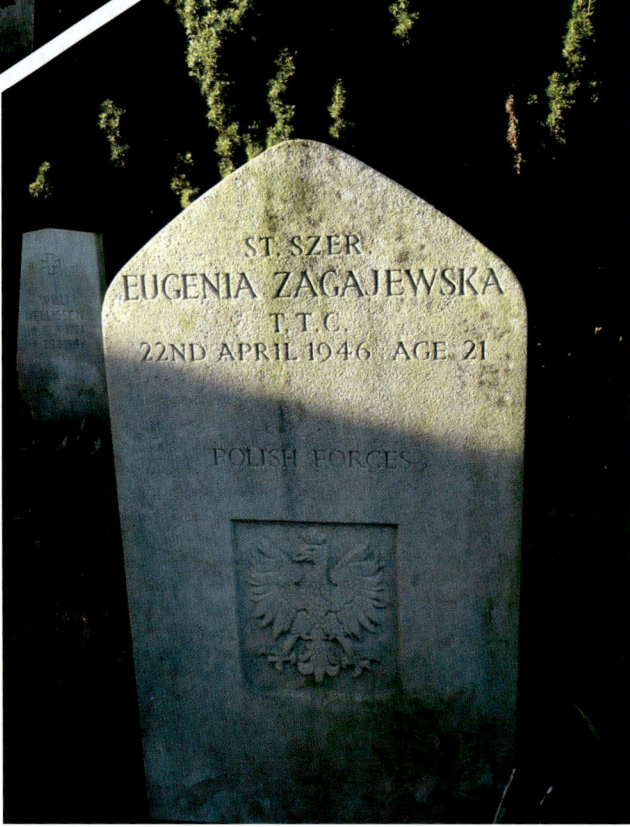

Masudi, Faustin and Vanueli

†2009

Masudi was born in 1968 in Kazimia and grew up on the banks of Lake Tanganyika in the Congo (DRC), surrounded by an extended family who all lived in his grandparents' house. Apart from looking after the animals and the crops (avocado, mango and banana trees), Masudi learned tailoring and preaching and became a Pastor in the Congolese Church like his father. He also liked to sing and make music. He met Sharon Chitambala, one of his father's parishioners and they married in the late 1990s just when the Congo was engulfed in a series of conflicts which sent them fleeing to Zambia. They stayed there seven or eight years in a refugee camp where their three children were born. They supported themselves, *Masudi* by making clothes and Sharon by working for the UN assisting fellow refugees. All these years *Masudi* and Sharon were dreaming of coming to Britain where they could give their children a good education. Finally in 2006 they arrived in Norwich. *Masudi* started an accountancy course, Sharon a NVQ in social work.

Some of their relatives had settled in Manchester and everyone was invited to a graduation ceremony there in July 2009. *Isengelo Masudi* (41), his friend *Faustin Patachako* (47) and his nephew *Vanueli Ramadhani* (25) took to the road but never arrived. They were killed in a car crash in Nottinghamshire on 17th July 2009. (Note 12).

KIBUNGU
VANUEL
RAMADHANI
Born 1st January 1984
Died 17th July 2009
Beloved brother of Faustin
Rest in peace

In loving memory of
my Husband &
wonderful Daddy
ISENGELO
EWISI
MASUDI
B. 01. 06. 1968 - D. 17. 07. 2009
R. I. P.

FAUSTIN
EMIDI
PATACHAKO
Evangeliste de
l'église protestante
du Congo
né 1 Janvier 196
décédé
17 Juillet 20
Beloved husband
and father
Je suis le
chemin la vérité
et la résurrection

Let their loved ones speak

Although some gravestones just show the name and date of death, most relatives also chose an epitaph as a reflection on life in general or more interestingly, the life of the departed. *In the midst of life, we are in death* is a *passe-partout* formula which doesn't tell us much but an epitaph which alludes to someone's sudden death, or long illness appeals to our compassion and gives it an extra interest:

William Greenacre May 31st 1888, aged 21
A sudden change and then I fell
no time to bid my friends farewell
the end you know, my grave you see,
prepare yourself to follow me

Mary Ann Tillett 1880, aged 49yrs
Day by day we saw her fade
and gently sink away
yet often in our hearts we prayed
that she might longer stay

A well-quoted part of the scriptures can give revealing and pertinent information to whoever can read between the lines, like *John Abel*'s epitaph (see page 30) or *George Nunn*'s where we cannot help but think of a possible suicide or the result of a drunken episode.

George Turner Nunn
Found drowned
February 25th 1897
aged 45 yrs

Let all the world be silent for
the Lord Himself shall judge.
Lord all pitying saviour blest
grant him thine eternal rest

It sounds as if he needed a lot of forgiveness.

Rather than using the Bible or selecting from a repertory of existing verses, a few people are moved to write their own personal epitaph and the best example of this is that of the Salvation Army treasurer Joshua Pearce, which reads more like a eulogy, therefore is very modern in conception.

His life was honest, his actions kind
His temper sweet, of Christian mind
Slow to anger, unwilling to offend
A loving husband and a faithful friend.

Apart from financial limitations, the choices people make when deciding on their relatives' last places of abode are dependent to a large extent on their personality, belief system and feelings at the time. To express themselves the Earlham relatives chose mostly conventionally accepted symbols e.g., a grief-stricken female form laying flowers on the ground or head in hand clutching a book to her heart.

A weeping willow, a hand holding the ribbon of life.

A resplendent crown for someone who looks forward to the joy of future resurrection and reunion rather than death and separation.

Roses galore in various stages of flowering: Three rambling ones for George Potter, a beloved father and grandfather who had nine sons and nine daughters. (Note 13)

A single rose for Robert Bryony.

And a whole bouquet for Ann Spinks.

Some symbols have an informative role as well as a symbolic one:
A little bird on a rose branch for someone who died young, like Agnes King.

Two hands clasped; husband and wife buried here.

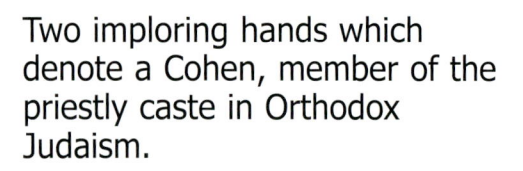

Two imploring hands which denote a Cohen, member of the priestly caste in Orthodox Judaism.

Two keys to eternity for Douro Potter who was also verger of St Peter Mancroft.

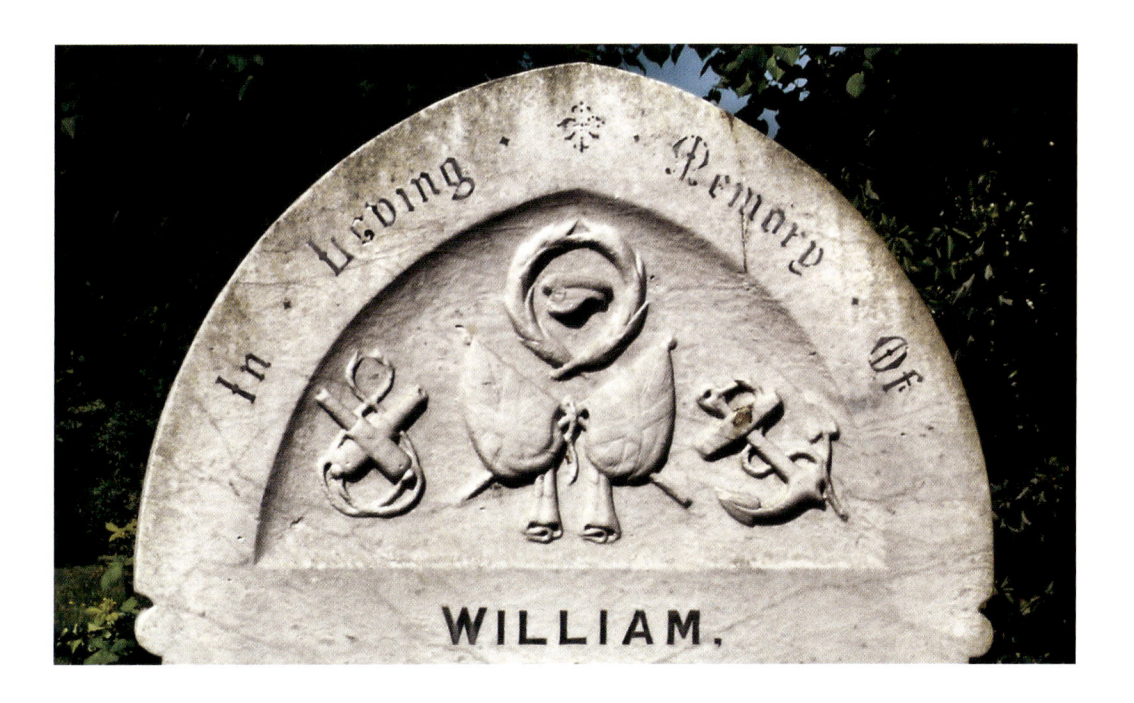

Flags, cannons and anchor for William Beckett, a gunner killed at sea, in combat.

A ship struggling in heavy seas for George Potter, who died on HMS Trafalgar.

The carving of the motifs as well as the quality of the stone itself, its shaping and the care taken over the lettering, can all combine to produce things of beauty which transcend their remit.

Beautifully carved inscriptions and a well chosen epitaph can be a powerful statement of grief, without additional decorations.

Had we been asked this we know
We should have cried Oh spare the blow
Yet with streaming tears should say
Lord we love her, let her stay.

Sometimes the pleasing effect is the random result of time and nature modifying the original human handiwork.

80

Like medieval bas-reliefs some works are there for our edification and wonderment, to be scrutinised and reflected upon.

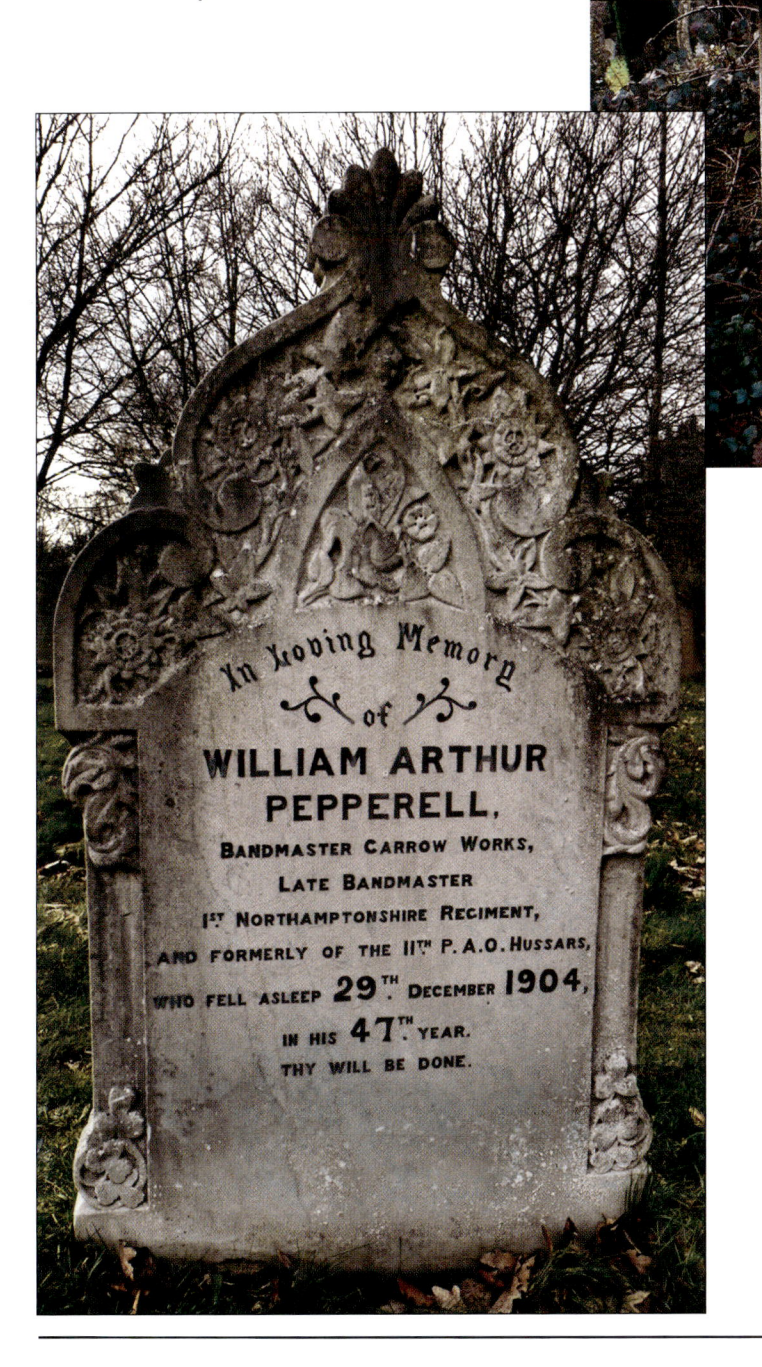

of
REBECCA
THE BELOVED WIFE OF
WILLIAM JOHN MUSK,
WHO DIED 3RD JULY 1899

Two angels holding crowns are framing the joined hands as if to lift them to Heaven.

A unique three dimensional depiction of a rather pagan looking female being, with delicately carved hands and feet, her hair dishevelled, floating in the air, holding a banner. Maybe she is an angel like all the others scattered around the graves, just looking happy.

"One to watch and one to pray
and two to bear my soul away..."

Conclusion

This piece of local research has come to an end, but this is a pause, not a conclusion; there are thousands of other gravestones in the cemetery clamouring to be rescued from oblivion and decay.

It is also a homage to the stonemasons who are the unsung artists working behind the scenes to keep the memory of the dead alive. They display their skills without any hope of recognition, quietly absorbing the styles of their epoch and integrating them into their designs, so much so that you can date a gravestone without looking at the inscription.

Let us hope that gravestone art will not disappear with the growth of memorial plaques and the widespread use of computer-aided designs.

After reading this book some readers might be inspired to go and look at the graves in situ. At the back of the book there is a map of the cemetery with a list of the graves marked in red on the map. Not all the graves are on the map. The numbers have been grouped into three possible circuits: graves 1 to 11, graves 12 to 20, and graves 21 to 26.

"Any man's death diminishes me, because I am involved in Mankind. And therefore never send to know for whom the bell tolls, it tolls for thee."

John Donne
(Note 14)

Notes

1 (p. 8)   *A short history of Earlham Cemetery* compiled by Jeremy Bartlett of the Friends of Earlham Cemetery.

2 (p. 9)   The Harvard Medical School study of Broken Heart Syndrome in the New England Journal of Medicine 2006.

3 (p. 10)   Shakespeare, William; Macbeth, Act IV, scene 3.

4 (p. 13)   Norfolk Annals, A Chronological Record of remarkable Events in the Nineteenth Century compiled by Charles MacKie; 'The Norfolk Chronicle' 31/03/1863.

5 (p. 35)   *Derby Vulliamy Clock*: Courtesy of Derby Museum. Derby Museum © 2013. A white marble mantel clock with ormolu allegorical details.

6 (p. 36)   *Justine Vulliamy Clock*: Image courtesy of Martin Gatto and Tavernicus. Wood lacquered in the Chinese style, England around 1795. The movement is a brass timepiece in the standard Vulliamy teardrop cased style. Justin later became a surgeon established in Rugby. A medical journal of the time refers to him being bilingual due to the fact that he was partly brought up in Normandy. Alice died in Ware at 39, unmarried, the same month as her mother. She made Justin her sole heir, sign of a closeness she didn't have with her other siblings.

7 (p. 44)   Quoted by J. Pound in Norwich in the 19th century, Chapter 2, edited by Christopher Barringer.

8 (p. 47)   Quoted by S. Cherry in Doing different? Politics and the Labour movement in Norwich 1880-1914.

9 (p. 48)   George Softley also plays a part in the life of Joshua Pearce.

10 (p. 56)   A contemporary account written by Basil Robert.

11 (p. 61)   see *Joshua Pearce*'s epitaph in the section *Let their loved ones speak.*

12 (p. 69)   Where there are variations for names I chose the version used by the family.

13 (p. 73)   He was Douro Potter's grandfather.

14 (p. 85)   John Donne Devotions upon Emergent Occasions, Meditation 17, 1624

Bibliography

Ancestry.co.uk
Barringer, Christopher (ed), Norwich in the nineteenth century, Gliddon Books, 1984. pg. 47-71.
Bury St Edmunds Record Office.
www.suffolkheritagedirect.org.uk.One-stop gateway to Suffolk Record Office's catalogues and Suffolk's heritage collections SROB/HC502/106 and SROB/HC502/108.

Cambridge University. 'Reproduced by kind permission of the Syndics of Cambridge University Library.' EAD/GBR/0012/MS Add.9839/1G correspondence between Newton and Goldsmith (for John Sayer). Pg. 342-346.

Chandler, Michael, Murder and crime in Norwich, The History Press, 2010. pg 50-58.
Cherry, Steven, Doing different? Politics and the Labour movement in Norwich, 1880-1914 , Centre of East Anglian Studies, 1989. Pg. 10,22,31-33,111.

Cotchin, Edward, The Royal Veterinary College, London: a bicentenary history, Barracuda Books, 1990. pg.27-29,67,87.
Eastern Daily Press.
HEART online www.heritagecity.org/research-centre.

Levine, Henry, The Norwich Hebrew Congregation 1840-1960.
Le Petit Français Illustré Armand Colin & Cie, 1895.
Loveday, Michael,The Norwich Knowledge, Michael Loveday 2011.

Mackie, Charles, Norfolk Annals, chronological record of remarkable events in the nineteenth century, volume II, 1851-1900, www.hellenicaworld.com/UK/literature/CharlesMackie/en/NorfolkAnnals2.html.

Meeres, Frank, Strangers – a history of Norwich's incomers , Norwich HEART, 2012, pg 113.
The National Archives. The nationalarchives.gov.uk.
Rutherford, Sarah, The Victorian cemetery, Shire Publications, 2008.

Picture credits

All the photos of graves are by the author except for the photograph of the John Abel stallion on the title page and pg.27 taken by Bill Smith and the following six which are by Jeremy Bartlett: James Self grave pg.8, Isaac Lazarus grave pg.8, Caley grave pg.21, Jarrolds Frieze pg.41, Sarah Rice top section of grave pg.48, Kiyoshi Hata grave pg.50. The rest of the illustrations are acknowledged below.

©Tate, London 2013: A detail from: Frontispiece to '*The Germ*' 1850; Hunt, William Holman (b 1827- D 1910). Etching on paper, Tate collection, presented by Edmund Houghton 1898 Ref. No 2422 pg.9.

© Mary Evans Picture Library / The Women's Library@LSE: Image: 10035132 What a woman may be, and yet not have the vote... pg.12
1002664 Elizabeth Garrett (later Anderson) (1836-1917) passes her doctoral examination at the Faculte de Medecine, Paris (France) - the first woman to do so, pg.12

The Granger Collection, New York: Image: 0090825 Christmas: Bell-ringing. The bow-bell peal on Christmas eve. Wood engraving, English, 1850. pg.16
0000926 Sino-Japanese war, 1894-5. The sinking of the Chinese ship Kow-Shing by Japanese men-of-war, July 1894. Illustration by a Chinese artist for an English newspaper, 1894 pg.65.

Image courtesy of Norfolk County Council library and information service: www.picture.norfolk.gov.uk: St. Peter Mancroft, Norwich, Stained glass window. Photographer Richard Tilbrook. With thanks to Roy Tricker Ref. NP00003485 pg.17.
The Caley Works at Chapel Field 1905. pg.19.
A.J. Caley Ltd. Norwich, Cracker manufacture NP00014660 (Bridewell Museum Ref. 4.599.3) pg.20.
Heigham Hall:Ref. NP00007479 pg.37.
Norfolk and Norwich Hospital pg.38.
Babies in a sun shelter at the Jenny Lind pg.47.
Elephants holding tails (Barnum Bailey Circus) pg.50.
Hardingham Hall: Mrs. John Edwards in a pony phaeton outside Ref: NP00000395 pg.62.

Norfolk Museums & Archeology Service: (Bridewell Museum)
Caley Cracker Advertisement pg.18.
Ladies boot made by Howlett and White Ltd Norwich (later Norvic) around 1900 pg.44.

By kind permission of Heckingham Hall: Red Poll Cattle, with thanks to Mr. NC and E Roberts www.heckingham-hall.co.uk pg.19.

Ernest Cotchin, The Royal Veterinary College, London. Barracuda Books Ltd 1990: Horse in the lecture theatre: pg 108. Pg.22; Notice pg 87 pg.24.

Look and Learn / Barbara Loe Collection: www.lookandlearn.com; Ponds dog pg.25.

Antique Engravings, Prints, Maps and Newspapers: stu@tds.net   John Abel; Roadster Stallion pg.30.

Norfolk Museums & Archeology Service: Servant pg.31.

1800 Woodcuts by Thomas Bewick and his school: Edited by Blanche Cirker, Dover Publications, Inc., New York: Cutler (turner) - Plate 176,2 pg.32; Woman washing clothes - Plate 165,5, pg.32; Plate 163,9, Finis pg.85 and 224,3 The End pg.92.

The Office of National Statistics Open License number 1.0: Enumeration slip pg.33.

Courtesy of Derby Museum: Vulliamy Clock: Derby Museum © 2013. pg.35

Image courtesy of Martin Gatto and Tavernicus: tavernicus@tavernicus.co.uk - image: Justine Vulliamy Clock pg.36.

© Erich Lessing/Erich Lessing Culture and Fine Arts Archive, Vienna: image: 40110366. Berthe Morisot, Le Berceau, 1872; Original painting held at Musée d'Orsay, Paris, France pg.39.

The Girl's Own Paper: Happy Old Age, October 6, 1894 pg.43.

Hampshire County Council Arts & Museums Service: Fan - image: BWM1967.516 DPAAHR24 pg.45.

© The British Library Board: Brought to Bed: Childbearing in America 1750-1950 (Oxford University Press, 1985), Judith Walzer Leavitt pg.105. Disclaimer: Efforts to establish copyright ownership of this image have proved unsuccessful. pg.46. Illustrated London News 19th September 1874. Rail disaster illustration pg. 63.

Courtesy of National Anthropological Archives, Smithsonian Institution: (INV 04637400) Man, drum and three child acrobats pg.49.

Dornier 217E-4: The Fernhurst Society (image), Dornier Museum Friedrichshafen. Disclaimer: Efforts to establish copyright ownership of this image have proved unsuccessful pg.51.

Peace Pledge Union: www.ppu.org.uk : WWI anti-war poster pg.55. Co group WWI Princetown Quarry pg.56.

Country and Eastern: with thanks to J. and P. Millward for the *Skating Rink* pg.58, Salvation Army diary entry pg.59 and 'Uncle Josh' photo pg.61.

Location map: after the original kindly supplied by Norwich City Council pg.90

Earlham Cemetery grave location guide.

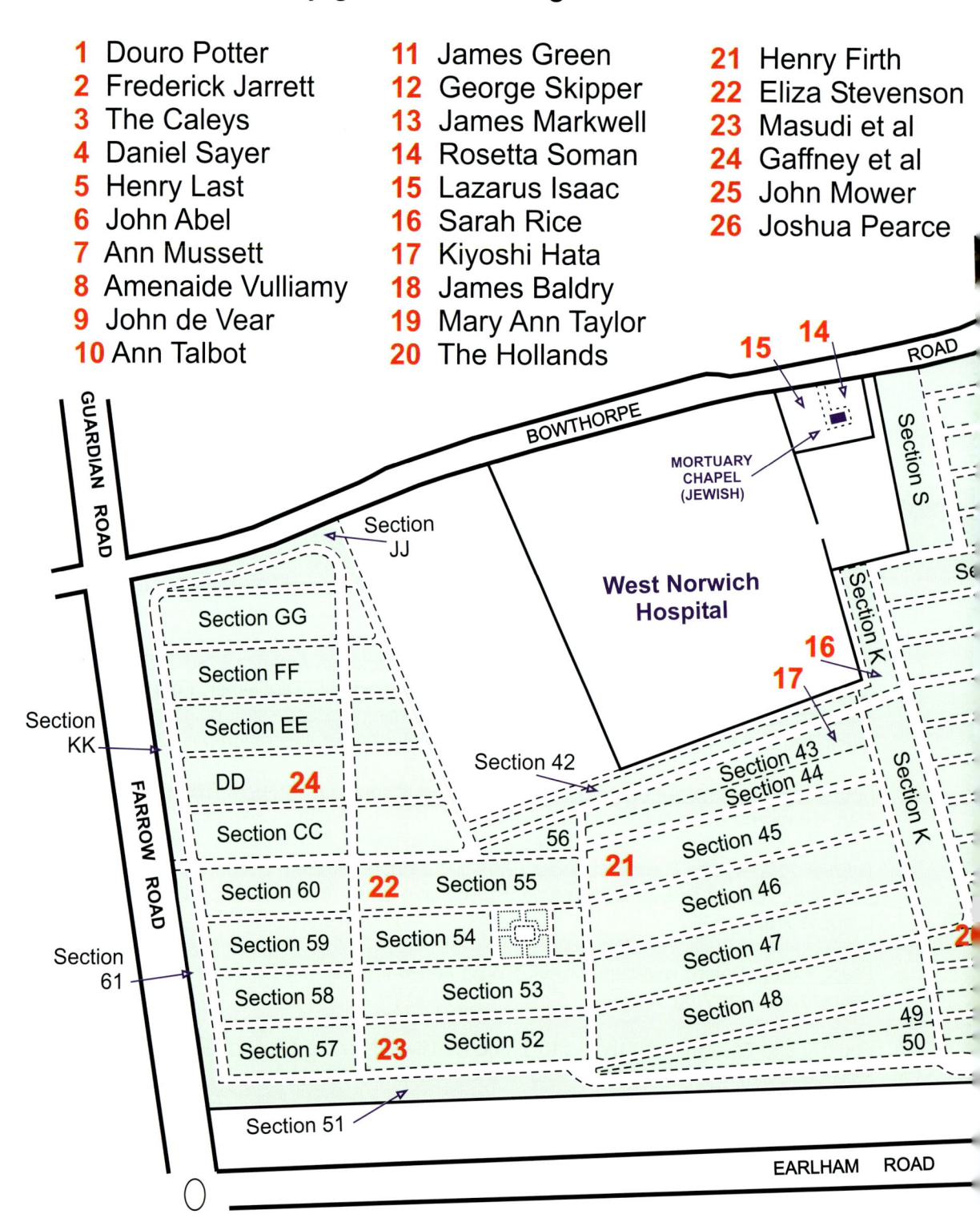

1. Douro Potter
2. Frederick Jarrett
3. The Caleys
4. Daniel Sayer
5. Henry Last
6. John Abel
7. Ann Mussett
8. Amenaide Vulliamy
9. John de Vear
10. Ann Talbot
11. James Green
12. George Skipper
13. James Markwell
14. Rosetta Soman
15. Lazarus Isaac
16. Sarah Rice
17. Kiyoshi Hata
18. James Baldry
19. Mary Ann Taylor
20. The Hollands
21. Henry Firth
22. Eliza Stevenson
23. Masudi et al
24. Gaffney et al
25. John Mower
26. Joshua Pearce

DEREHAM ROAD
MAIN DRIVE
BURIAL CHAPEL
CREMATORIUM
R.C. CHAPEL
OFFICE
Section P
Section J
Section B
Section A
Section T
Section U
Section V
Section W
Section X
Section Y
Section AA
BB
Section Z
Section 41
Section 1
Section 2
Section 3
Section 4
Section 5
Section 6
Section 7
Section 8
Section 9
Section 10
Section 11
N

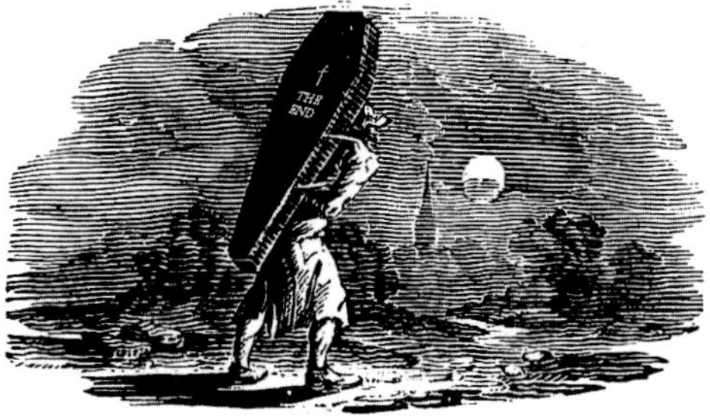
THE
END

Reader's notes

Reader's notes

Reader's notes